Augustine on the Body

American Academy of Religion Dissertation Series

edited by
H. Ganse Little, Jr.

Number 31

Augustine on the Body
by
Margaret Ruth Miles

Margaret Ruth Miles

Augustine on the Body

Scholars Press

Distributed by
Scholars Press
PO Box 5207
Missoula, Montana 59806

Augustine on the Body
Margaret Ruth Miles

Library of Congress Cataloging in Publication Data

Miles, Margaret Ruth.
Augustine on the body.

(Dissertation series - American Academy of Religion ; no. 31)
Bibliography: p.
1. Man (Christian theology) 2. Augustinus, Aurelius, Saint, Bp. of Hippo—Theology. 3. Body, Human (in religion, folk-lore, etc.) I. American Academy of Religion. II. Title. III. Series: American Academy of Religion. Dissertation Series - American Academy of Religion ; no. 31.
BT701.2.M53 233 79-14226
ISBN 0-89130-288-3
ISBN 0-89130-289-1 pbk.

Printed in the United States of America

1 2 3 4 5 6

Edwards Brothers, Inc.
Ann Arbor, MI 48104

TABLE OF CONTENTS

ACKNOWLEDGMENTS

I wish to express my gratitude to Professor Massey Shepherd for his continual help and encouragement; from his great personal kindness in helping me with Latin when I began the doctoral program to his scholarly generosity in making suggestions of the greatest importance concerning the dissertation, his help has been invaluable. I also warmly acknowledge Professor Matthew Evans, chairman of the Humanities Department at San Francisco State University, who first stimulated my interest in what has been an exciting and personally fruitful study. My appreciation goes to Professor Peter Brown, author of the first biography of Augustine I read, later my mentor and friend, the generous source of support and important suggestions. The members of my dissertation committee, Professor Dorothy Donnelly and Professor Gerard Caspary, whose time and energy I have been receiving through most of the period of my doctoral study, I thank with continuing appreciation. And I wish to thank my parents, Dr. and Mrs. Kenneth L. Miles, for the quality and quantity of their loving encouragement.

Finally--although these acknowledgments do not begin to exhaust the names of those who have contributed a rich variety of gifts to this project--I am thankful for the motivating gift of delight in this study, for, as Peter Brown has said, "it is just this vital capacity to engage one's feelings on a course of action, to take delight in it, that escapes our powers of self-determination." Augustine described the mystery of motivation by delight accurately and economically:

"Inardescimus et imus."

--<u>Confessions</u> XIII.9

M.R.M.

Berkeley, 1977

CHAPTER I

INTRODUCTION

"Sanitas autem perfecta corporis illa extrema totius hominis immortalitas erit."

Epistula CXVIII.3.14

The problem of formulating a description of the relationship of mind and body which adequately accounts for both experiential data and the requirements of systematic thought is the decisive problem of human thought; a changed description requires fundamental and painful reorientations of energy and value. The stone which the classical builders had rejected in their conceptual edifice was the body; but, in the manner which Freud has elucidated for us, a denial is simultaneously an affirmation, a *focus* which gives the lie to its intellectual negation and evidences itself psychologically as ambivalence, frustration, and eventually sterility in thought and action.[1] If, as Norman O. Brown has suggested, the goal of human culture is the integration of the repressed, Augustine's struggle to describe the meaning and value of the human body is a decisive stage in this common goal. Seen as a segment of a process, a segment which we isolate and spotlight only in order to indicate its importance within and to the process, Augustine's formulation follows the work of analysis and exploration of the components of human being which classical thought had articulated. The excitement and energy of the discovery of a distinction between body process and mind-as-process[2] is most clearly seen in Aristotle's careful analysis of the specific function of mind in the *Nichomachean Ethics*. In these pages one still senses the tremendous surcharge of freedom carried by the discovery that the proper function of mind is theoretically and functionally distinguishable from its physical ground.[3] To distinguish is not to separate, but the dynamic tension required to hold together mind-as-process and body process is overwhelmingly difficult to sustain; the human temptation is to break the tension of integration in favor of one component. Classical thought valued the mind with the result that the body, the denied or repressed component, was left to "return" negatively and regressively in such cultural phenomena as the popular demand for entertainment featuring sex and violence--the symptom in every age of inadequate integration of the body--and the astonishing social wastefulness of slavery.

The classical model of the human person is that of a mixture of soul and body; its method of description and ethical action is analysis and hierarchical evaluation of these components. The Christian model, on the other hand, is that of a unity; its method is relative valuation, or ordering, of the members of the unity. In Christian thought the body achieves a radically new significance, not only explicitly in the doctrines of the Incarnation and the resurrection of the body, but implicitly as a metaphor for the Church. The idea of mixture was deeply troubling both to classical (Stoic and Neoplatonic) and to dualist (Gnostic-Manichaean) thought. It described an experience of contamination of the higher by the lower elements.

Simone Pétrement has usefully distinguished between metaphysical dualism and felt dualism, "the feeling of being something double, a contradiction."[4] Metaphysical dualism is the conceptual formulation of this experience: "it's not because two worlds or two principles have been conceived, that the necessity of a difficult passage and a profound change has been affirmed, but it is because this passage and this change have been affirmed that two worlds have been imagined."[5] Stoic and Neoplatonic thought remains close to felt dualism in that although this experience is never given a full metaphysical articulation, it emerges strongly in the ethical teachings of both schools.[6] In Gnostic-Manichaean tradition, metaphysical dualism is fully formulated and it may be that the experience of disjunction and mixture is overshadowed and partially lost in the metaphysical emphasis.[7]

An appropriate metaphor for the classical task of distinguishing mind and body is provided by Jung's study of medieval treatises on alchemy. These treatises describe the necessity of differentiation of alchemical elements as a paradigm for the first stage of coming to selfhood. Consciousness, Jung says, is the perception of differences. The *unio naturalis*, or undifferentiated totality, described by the alchemists as "chaos . . . mutual contamination," which characterizes the unexamined life, must move through the several stages of analysis to synthesis, or differentiated unity.[8] The classical attempt to distinguish or analyze the components of human being is thus seen as the necessary first stage in becoming fully human; Jung writes, "The alchemists rightly regarded 'mental union in the overcoming of the body' as only the first stage of conjunction or individuation."[9] The classical intuition that this task of differentiation was indeed the task of the time was strong, and marked a tremendous advance in human consciousness.

But the absolutizing of the task by classical and dualist thinkers led to the neglect of the next task, that of the reunion of soul and body. This task was the primary emphasis of patristic authors, that is, "keeping body and soul together"; on the intellectual level, the defense of the Christian formulation of the experience of history and revelation, which accounted for the fact that human being has to do irreducibly with physical being, and on the level of action, the struggle to discover genuinely Christian values, values which integrate body and soul. Tertullian stated it thus, "If the flesh is not God's creation, if it was not really sanctified by the Incarnation, and if it can have no part in eternal life, then it is a thing of no account . . . and it then seems to be a matter of opinion whether it should be maltreated with excessive rigorism or equally maltreated by allowing it unbridled license."[10] But it is precisely these aspects of Christian revelation that the patristic writers must explain and support again and again; these dogmas require a wholistic anthropology, an integration of the body.

It is important to remember that late classical people, pagan and Christian, had a great deal in common with each other;

the experience of discomfort with being in a body appears in Christian thought because patristic writers are classical men, not because it is characteristically Christian. Although a dualistic anthropology is certainly evident in Paul, it is always an existential dualism from which no metaphysical absolutes are drawn.[11] To the extent that a patristic author has understood the significance of the Incarnation and the Resurrection of Christ, he will insist on the meaning and value of the human body; insofar as these doctrines have not permeated his consciousness and values, he will write as a late classical author, demonstrating the negative valuation of the body characteristic of the culture. Thus, we find Ambrose, for example, using the classical model for the human composite: the soul, he writes in De bono mortis 26, is our "true substance" and the "superior element" ought not to be mixed or confounded with the inferior element, the body.

In attempting, then, to illuminate Augustine's anthropology from the angle of his idea of the relationship of body and soul, many obvious and also several subtle influences must be taken into account. The obvious influences include classical philosophy, especially Stoic and Neoplatonic philosophy, Gnostic-Manichaean tradition, in which Augustine spent nearly a decade of his formative youth, and finally, Scripture and patristic writers. Stoic philosophy, already long past its peak of creative and energetic thought in Augustine's time, provided the climate of opinion which was Augustine's environmental and educational heritage in addition to specific ideas. Gnostic-Manichaean tradition perhaps contributed most to Augustine's development by its choice of problems, a negative focus on the body that Augustine was to combat until his death.[12]

The Neoplatonists, Plotinus and Porphyry, with whose works Augustine's familiarity has been painstakingly demonstrated,[13] were among the most important and lasting of Augustine's influences. His excitement with the discovery of Neoplatonic thought, well attested in the Confessions and variously evaluated by reviewers, seems to have been the bridge which connected Augustine with Catholic Christianity. If the metaphor of the bridge is misleading in indicating that once crossed, the bridge becomes useless, we should allow that there was more mileage than that in Neoplatonism for Augustine. The extent of Neoplatonic influence on Augustine's Catholic Christianity, especially in the critical area of the relationship of mind and body, must be analyzed very closely; it is pivotal. For while both Stoics and Neoplatonists can be found advising an attempt to "escape from the fetters of the body as from a prison," the Neoplatonic formulation is a far more articulate and subtle treatment of this relationship, a treatment which Augustine never ceased to respect.

Finally, the formulations of the earlier Catholic fathers, especially those who participated in the Antiochean and Alexandrian schools, will be discussed. It will be seen that the preoccupation of both apologetic and didactic writing was consistently elucidation of those aspects of the Christian faith that require a new evaluation of the human body. In addition, these authors illuminate the difficulty of a specifically Christian evaluation of the body in their teachings on martyrdom and asceticism. In examining the teachings on the doctrinal formulas concerning Incarnation and resurrection, we can catch the conscious intellectual aspect of their thinking on the body; in the teachings on martyrdom and asceticism, we can uncover indications of their difficulty with integrating properly Christian evaluations. The influence of Scripture and patristic authors became more and more central to Augustine after his ordination as a bishop; he quoted Ambrose more frequently than any other Christian writer except Cyrpian, whom he quoted extensively for polemical purposes in the Donatist controversy.

The more subtle influences are more difficult to document and describe. One of the most important has already been mentioned: the extent to which any individual participates in the mutually constructed consciousness of his culture and age. It has been estimated that "even strong personalities are sixty to eighty percent the result of their environment, about twenty to forty percent representing their personal contribution. Feeble personalities . . . are ninety to ninety-nine percent their environment."[14] Augustine was assuredly a strong personality; yet even if we arbitrarily assign the sixty percent figure to environmental influence, we can see that the influence is still very strong.

Secondly, we cannot neglect to take into account the stage at which a person makes certain kinds of conceptual formulations; the kind of statement which a person makes concerning the meaning and value of the body will have to do very intimately with how old he is. One example will suffice: Simone Pétrement has noticed the curious coincidence of a dualistic tendency in Plato, most pronounced in youth and recurring in old age, which rather closely recalls a similar phenomenon in the life of Augustine, a concentration of dualistic emphasis in youth and old age: the young Manichee became the old predestinarian.[15] This is curious, and of more than passing interest. Does dualistic thought tend to dominate, especially among "intellectuals," in those stages of life in which human beings are especially identified with their bodies--in youth and again in old age when bodily pains and limitations become a governing factor on possibilities for activity?

It is difficult to know how much weight to put on such intangible and undocumented influences; our own degree of self-awareness and understanding is the only indication. In addition, Augustine himself has not taken into account that different stages of life have different tasks, and that growth and insight at any particular stage largely depends on the extent to which the tasks of the previous stage are accomplished. Augustine nowhere shows himself to be aware of what his mature understanding of self and world owes to his intellectual, emotional, and sexual activities at earlier stages. While the Confessions certainly demonstrate Augustine's awareness of process, yet they make no attempt to evaluate the stages of his holistic development in terms of the valuable 'learning for oneself' that characterized them.

Finally, we are left to conjecture how much of Augustine's personal temperament has 'colored' his Christian teaching. An enormously difficult factor to evaluate, the effect of Augustine's temperament may be 'minimized' as the commitment, common to many late classical men, to evaluate themselves and their environment rather harshly in order to choose, in order not to fall into the unthinking habits of their fellows. Or, the effect of Augustine's temperament may be 'maximized' as Guitton has done:

> . . . we may wonder to what degree Christianity still suffers from St. Augustine's pessimism, which is explicable by his temperament, the circumstances of his passionate and brooding youth, and his nine years association with the Manichaeans. Why should a people bear permanently the image of what . . . a single individual once underwent?[16]

These influences need to be interwoven in any account of Augustine's ideas. My method will be to attempt to do so in the process of discussing Augustine's anthropology under four categories which I take to illuminate different aspects of this anthropology. The categories are: (1) his theory of sensation, (2) his ascetic teachings, (3) his teaching on the Incarnation, and (4) his teaching on the resurrection of the body. I have chosen these categories both for their obvious relevance and because the doctrinal statements and explanations given by Augustine in his lengthy career as a Christian teacher demonstrate the extent of his conscious integration of genuinely Christian values, while his theory of sensation and teaching on asceticism show the unconscious aspect of his thought which still participates in classical tasks and images. I will support the thesis that Augustine's development in these areas moves from the tendency to view the body as the ground of existential alienation to affirmation of the whole person. The following quotations indicate a complex and subtle intellectual development, a change in emphasis, which we will observe; first, from the _Soliloquia_ of the Cassiciacum period:

> There is but one thing I can teach thee; I know nothing more. These things of the senses are to be utterly shunned and the utmost care must be used lest while we bear this body our wings be impeded by their snare; seeing that we need them whole and perfect if we would fly from this darkness to that light, which deigns not even show itself to those shut up in the cage of the body unless they have been such that whether it were broken through or dissolved they would escape into air which was theirs.[17]

From _In Joannis Evangelium tractatus_ XXVII.5:

> It is said, 'the flesh profiteth nothing' . . . but this means of itself. Let the spirit be added to the flesh, as charity is added to knowledge, and it profiteth much. For if the flesh profiteth nothing,

> the Word had not been made flesh that it might dwell in us. If through the flesh Christ hath greatly profited us, how does the flesh profit nothing? But it is through the flesh that the spirit acted for our salvation. . . . For how should the sound of the Word reach us except through the voice of the flesh?[18]

Yet the study of a conscious intellectual struggle to integrate an ignored or repressed aspect is partial to the point of distortion if it totally ignores the unconscious resistance which inevitably accompanies such an increment of consciousness. We will see areas in which Augustine betrays ambivalence and incomplete integration. The data--Augustine's own writings--must not be clarified to the extent of oversimplifying his struggle, his perplexity, his process, a process both multidimensional and rich--which leads, in Augustine's old age to predestinarianism and harsh statements concerning the body's most intimate function, sexuality--as surely as it leads to systematic intellectual integration of the body. We will be dealing not only with a conscious linear development, but also with a subtly interwoven countermotion of unconscious resistance. Although the bulk of our study will deal with Augustine's conscious integration of the body, we will be careful to acknowledge the points at which his ambivalence expresses itself.

Texts from the Cassiciacum and priesthood period will be compared with texts from Augustine's maturity and older age in an attempt to grasp not only the import of the statements made, but also the 'flavor' or emphasis given to these statements in the total work. Although Augustine's statements concerning the body show a degree of homogeneity from the first of his Christian career to the end of his life, there is a shift of accent which is very significant. Rejecting Gilson's statement[19] that Augustine was not interested in a systematic description of the function of the body, I think we can show his central conscious concern with the stone which the classical builders had rejected. Just as Robinson has demonstrated that Paul's use of 'body' was pivotal in his theology, we can show that, from the 390s on, under the increasing knowledge and influence of Scripture Augustine was pivotally concerned to integrate his idea of the meaning and value of the body with his philosophical and dogmatic persuasions.

CHAPTER II

THE DEVELOPMENT OF AUGUSTINE'S THEORY OF SENSATION FROM THE CASSICIACUM DIALOGUES TO DE CIVITATE DEI XXII

"Quid est sanitas? . . . Ergo non sic sentire, ut non sentit lapis, ut non sentit arbor, ut non sentit cadaver; sed vivere in corpore, et nihil ex ejus onere sentire, hoc est sanum esse."

Serm. CCLXXVII.5-6

i

A close study of St. Augustine's description of sensation is pivotal to an understanding of his idea of the meaning and value of the body. Unfortunately, the most perceptive of Augustinian scholars agree that his theory of sensation is riddled with inconsistencies and difficulties. This chapter will proceed by discussing Augustine's theory of sensation in two stages of his intellectual and spiritual development, that of the early Dialogues, most systematically elucidated in *De musica* VI, and his mature description, centering in *De Genesi ad litteram* XII and, less fully treated, in *De Trinitate* XI. I have found only one abbreviated and generalized developmental treatment of Augustine's understanding of sensation[1] and although I do not claim that a developmental treatment entirely clarifies the irreducible ambiguities in his thought on sensation, it is hopelessly distorting to amalgamate into one theory of sensation Augustine's self-acknowledged process of understanding. When we have treated it developmentally--and only then--we will be justified in differentiating between consciously articulated difficulties within a systematic exposition of sensation, and unconscious, unexamined assumptions which underlie his description and render it ambiguous. I will examine Augustine's theory of sensation in two stages because I do not find it changed or modified in its theoretical aspect in Augustine's later life. Rather, he increasingly uses--makes concrete and operative--what he has outlined theoretically in his mature writings. Thus the later Augustine's practical pastoral use of the role of sensation will be examined briefly in the last section.

The background of Augustine's early understanding of sensation was almost completely secular and philosophical. This remains largely true of his mature theory; Scripture does not solve the question and the earlier patristic writers discuss it only cursorily in attempts to elucidate the participation of two natures in one human being as a paradigm of the Incarnation.

Augustine's early interest in describing sensation arose from the attempt to describe, in the Cassiciacum dialogues, the nature of human life in the body. Not only is the problem itself philosophic, with a background of treatment by Stoics, Epicureans, Peripatetics, Skeptics, and Middle and Neoplatonists, but the assumptions and arguments used are drawn from these earlier philosophical discussions.

It is important to notice the context in which Augustine finds it necessary to describe sensation in the dialogues. Like Plotinus, Augustine discusses sensation in the context of discussions on the impassibility of the soul. His theory of sensation is used to demonstrate the grandeur and power of the soul. This is significant, and it is often overlooked when Augustine's theory of the relationship of body and soul is characterized. The oversimplification of an idea is always marked by this lifting out of context, by its isolation from both the question it was designed to address and the other answers to this question which it was designed to refute. Perhaps its significance can be indicated best by Peter Brown's suggestion in another context: "If you were traveling on a train and met, and were speaking with Mani, could you get more mileage out of him by asking him about the worthlessness of his body or the grandeur of his soul?"[2] The point is that if the theme is the worthlessness of the body, one can expect to find a careful discussion of the exact extent and limit of this 'worthlessness,' the point at which one adds, "But oh! how beautifully constructed and valuable it is in spite of its not being the _highest_ value." If, however, the theme is the grandeur of the soul, one can expect to see the body used merely as a _contrast_ to this grandeur. It is in this latter context that Plotinus and Augustine discuss sensation. With this consideration in mind, then, let us begin to describe Augustine's theory of sensation as a subdivision of his idea of the significance of the soul.

Sensation, in Augustine's scheme, is the lowest, that is, the most basic, form of knowledge; it is first in the order of discovery and, for that reason, last in the order of value. In fact, it cannot, with complete accuracy, be designated 'knowledge' because it operates on objects of flagrant mutability. Augustine speaks of sensation not as a product, but as an activity. Not even for purposes of distinction can an act of sensing be considered solely in its physical aspect; rather, sensation is the act of a soul using its body as a musician uses his instrument: "Tell me, in what sense does the soul use the body for sensing?"[3]

In insisting on the soul's activity in sensation, Augustine is following Plotinus' rejection of Aristotle's teachings concerning sensation, and also that of the Epicureans and the Stoics, who had all "understood sensation in a passive sense. They thought that the soul received impressions from the senses."[4] The Stoics and Epicureans used the word 'impressions' in a literal and physical sense; Aristotle's use was metaphorical.[5] The Stoic treatment of sensation occurs in the context of their discussion of knowledge. Sense impressions form the basis and content of knowledge; the mind, blank at birth, is imprinted with sense impressions.[6] The Stoic doctrine of πνεῦμα, the basic physical component of the universe which links all parts of the universe in a material contact or energy, guarantees the reality of the external objects which cause impressions to occur in the mind. "Intelligence is shaped and developed by the general concepts . . . [made up of] repeated records of the same thing or type of thing . . . which a man 'naturally' builds up from his primary sense experiences."[7] The Stoics then proceeded to draw a sharp distinction between impressions, passively received, and an active state which follows, not necessarily temporally in the case of any particular occasion, but logically--the "interpretation of the impression by discursive articulate thought."[8]

We will stop at this juncture of the Stoic account of sense perception because it is this stage of their account that concerns us here. Two aspects of the Stoic theory of sensation disturbed Augustine as they had Plotinus, and Augustine follows Plotinus' correction of these points in the early dialogues.

First, Augustine makes a sharp distinction between the object perceived and the sensation we have of it. 'Sensation' has entirely to do with the soul; the objects of sensation have entirely to do with body. The distinction is important to Augustine because it forms the basis of his criticism of (1) materialism and (2) passivity in the theory of sensation.

Plotinus, rejecting both the Stoics' and the Epicureans' materialistic theories of sensation in which sense perceptions are described as body acting on body, and the Aristotelian view that the soul is the form of the body,[9] described sensation as the soul's action "in harmony with" the body:

> Now if sensations of the active order depend upon the complement of soul and body, sensation must be of that double nature. Hence it is classed as one of the shared acts: the soul, in the feeling, may be compared to the workman in such operations as boring or weaving, the body to the tool employed: the body is passive and menial; the soul is active, reading such impressions as are made upon the body or discerned by means of the body . . . sensation is a shared task.[10]

The soul, since it is a substance in its own right and can exist independently of the body, possesses a categorical superiority over the body. This absolute hierarchical value of the soul means to Plotinus that the soul stands closer to participation in the One and therefore contains a greater increment of reality in contrast to the body so that it is not accessible to the action or influence of its inferior; the body, participating in an attenuated being due to the admixture of matter on which it is based[11] can never affect or operate on the soul.[12] Any influence between body and soul must proceed from the higher to the lower.[13]

In addition, for Plotinus the possibility of a cooperation between body and soul needed careful explanation. For the Stoics, such a possibility depended on the materiality of both soul and body; in fact, Cleanthes and Lucretius argued for the corporeality of the soul from the fact that it was affected by the body.[14] The two modes in which bodies might mingle without confusion had been distinguished by the Stoics as κρᾶσις (mixing) and παράθεσις (juxtaposition); neither of these allowed for the possibility of a unity of corporeal and incorporeal elements. The Neoplatonists had adopted a third possibility precisely in order to describe the union of soul and body: unio inconfusa: ἄμικτος ἀσύγχυτος ἕνωσις. This theory, which apparently originated with Ammonius Saccas,[15] maintained that "the union of intelligible entities with the body takes place without substantial alteration or intermixture on their part; as a parallel he instanced the union of light with air."[16] "It is absurd to class the living being as neither body nor soul; these two things cannot so change as to make a distinctive third, nor can they blend so utterly that the soul shall become a mere potentiality in the animated whole." Apparently, for Plotinus, the unio inconfusa description answered both his concern to refute Stoic materialism and the passive theory of sensation in which soul is acted upon by body and ultimately derives its knowledge and experience from the passive imprinting by the body and the external world. Rather, "the soul gives the body a share in her own life."[17]

Let us look briefly, for example, at Plotinus' account of vision. In Ennead III.6.1, Plotinus defines sensations, not as passive states, but as judgments.[18]

> In any perception we attain by sight, the object is grasped there where it lies in the direct line of vision; . . . the mind looks outward; this is ample proof that it has taken and takes no inner imprint, and does not see in virtue of some mark made upon it like that of the ring on the wax; it need not look outward at all if, even as it looked, it already held the image of the object, seeing by virtue of an impression made upon itself . . . most convincing of all, if to see is to accept imprints of the object of our vision, we can never see these objects themselves; we see only vestiges they leave within us, shadows; the things themselves would be very different from our vision of them. And, for a conclusive consideration, we cannot see if the living object is in contact with the eye; we must look from a certain distance; this must be more applicable to the mind; supposing the mind to be stamped with an imprint of the object, it could not grasp as an object of vision what is stamped upon itself. . . . But if perception does not go by impression, what is the process? The mind affirms something not contained within itself; this is precisely the characteristic of a

> power--not to accept impression but, within its allotted sphere, to act.[19]

We find three aspects of Plotinus' refutation of the Stoic theory of sensation which will concern us in our exploration of Augustine's explanation of sensation: rejection of materialism, rejection of passivity, and, finally, the value of sensation in Plotinus' hierarchy of values. Augustine follows Plotinus in his concern in the dialogues to describe the interaction of body and soul in a way that rejects materialism and passivity. He also stresses the superiority of the soul over the body as Plotinus had, and the way in which a focus of attention on the needs of the body distracts the soul from its search for truth.[20] We will proceed to describe Augustine's theory of sensation by exploring his use of these Plotinian objections.

What does Augustine think the soul is? Accustomed as we are to assume that the idea of the spirituality of the soul is inseparable from Christianity, we tend to ignore the fact that this idea of the soul was not established until a relatively late date. Numenius and Ammonius, who heavily influenced Neoplatonism, deduced the spirituality of the soul from the fact that it 'contains' the body, a role which only an immaterial principle is capable of assuming. A unifying principle is necessary --a principle which could not be another body.[21] Since Neoplatonic and other writers had characterized the soul as immaterial and therefore immortal, some ecclesiastical writers, among them Tertullian, had vigorously denied the spirituality of the soul rather than assent to its divinity. Even in the fifth century, a number of ecclesiastical writers still taught that the human soul was material.[22] The Alexandrian fathers, however, used the Middle Platonists' argument to argue for the spirituality and immortality of the soul.[23] Augustine followed Ambrose in affirming the Alexandrian view while insisting at the same time on the soul's creatureliness in relation to God.[24]

The soul is, in addition, *active* in sensation. In his careful discussion of sensation in *De quantitate animae*, Augustine begins with a definition which assimilates sensation to a *passio*, an awareness by the mind of what the body experiences.[25] Without the attention of the soul, the body would be as if anesthetized. Gareth Matthews has described the Augustinian definition of soul and body; the soul is:

> an entity whose activities underlie the being and behavior of the body in such a way as to make the difference between merely physical activity, and the conscious, animated, purposive behavior characteristic of living human beings.

The body is:

> the 'part' of a man that is buried at death. It has physical characteristics and may be moved in various ways. But no psychological predicates may be applied to its behavior.[26]

"Both the images associated with particular sensations and the intellectual ideas corresponding to them are brought into being by the activity of the soul."[27] The soul, attentive to the modifications of its body, makes from its awareness of these modifications images which correspond to them. This is, in fact, the primary function of sensation:

> not to picture for the mind what things are like, but to warn the soul of changes in the body. . . . Instead of being in the body to suffer and receive, the soul is there to act and to give.[28]
>
> Since the soul cannot receive sensation ready-made from without, it must derive it from itself and, consequently, must give something of its own substance to form it."[29]

When, on the other hand, we do not pay attention to a sensation that is available to the senses, it is correct to say that no sensation occurs:

> And from this it often comes about, being occupied with another thought, we do not in conversation seem to have heard even ourselves. This is not because the soul does not at that time put in motion those reacting numbers, since certainly the sound reaches the ears, and the soul cannot be idle at its body's passion and since it cannot move differently than if that passion of the body should occur, but because the impetus of the motion is immediately blotted out by the attention on something else, an impetus which, if it remained, would remain in the memory so we would also know and feel we heard.[30]

Indeed, in De musica VI.4.7 Augustine says that it is not a question of being amazed at the soul's active role in sensation.[31] This absolute transcendence of soul over body, axiomatic for Augustine, requires that he describe sensation without allowing any action to be imposed on the mind by the bodily senses: "Augustine apparently envisioned [the soul's] awareness of bodily states as a kind of awareness by the mind of variations in the conditions of its operation."[32]

An interesting aspect of the intellectual relationship between Plotinus and Augustine comes to light when we compare Augustine's theory of vision with that of Plotinus. We have seen how Plotinus used the theory of vision to reject any possibility of passive sensation; distance, he argued, is absolutely necessary between the viewer and the object viewed, if any act of sight is to occur. If the impression were stamped on the soul, it could neither see it, nor make judgments of distance. Although Augustine agreed with Plotinus that the soul plays an active role in sensation, he strangely did not take advantage of Plotinus' arguments against the passive theory. Perhaps this was because Augustine did not know the portion of the Enneads in which these objections were discussed.[33] In any case, Augustine describes vision in De quantitate animae, by the ray theory: "the eye emits a ray of light which brings the sense organ into immediate contact with the object."[34] Plotinus had explicitly rejected the ray theory in Ennead III.6.1. Yet Augustine writes: "sight goes forth, and through the eye shines forth to light up what we see. Hence it follows that there it sees where the object is which it sees, and not at the point where it goes out to see."[35] Instead of using Plotinus' theory, Augustine adopts the Stoic theory of πνεῦμα which sheds its light on sensible objects, illuminating them so that perception can take place.[36] The activity of the soul in sensation, then, would be organic, inferior to, and an aspect of the bodily function, separable only conceptually.[37]

In fact, Augustine's concern, in the Cassiciacum dialogues, seems to have been to integrate Neoplatonic and Stoic descriptions of sensation rather than to argue for one or the other. Robert J. O'Connell has demonstrated Augustine's preoccupation in this period with showing the agreement of Stoic and Neoplatonic thinkers on the nature of human happiness; in De libero arbitrio, Augustine was trying "to combine the Stoic interest in the 'good will' in achieving the good life with the Neoplatonic intellectual quest for vision."[38] He "refused to view Stoicism and Neoplatonism as contradictories."[39] To carry O'Connell's thesis a bit further: in De musica VI, Augustine was attempting to combine the Neoplatonic spiritualistic interpretation of the activity of sensation with the Stoic doctrine of πνεῦμα. Michel Spanneut has also demonstrated that it is wrong to speak of Stoic materialism as opposed to spiritualism, that, in the epoch of the Church fathers, "Our antithesis of body and spirit did not exist. The fathers did not ask themselves the questions we ask about the relationship of body and spirit."[40] Stoic 'materialism' is characterized by Spanneut thus: "Matter is animated by the λόγος; of the union of matter and λόγος, body is formed. Thus, everything material is body, not because of feeble matter, but because of the animating λόγος." We do not have accounts of sensation in the writings of the Church fathers before Augustine because they tended to view matter and λόγος as inseparable, in analysis as well as in fact, according to the Stoic account which, as cultivated men of their time, they inherited from their intellectual milieu. The problem occurred when Neoplatonism attempted to describe how a spiritual substance can be 'housed' in an animated body. It only, in fact, became a recognized problem in Augustine's time when Neoplatonism had become the dominant philosophy. The earlier fathers, "rightly or wrongly," as Spanneut cautiously writes, "associated the Gnostic-dualistic heresies with Platonism, and combatted this dualism whether it was understood as between God and man, body and soul, or within the soul in its different modes of knowledge."[41] At a time when Gnosticism was the most threatening adversary of the Christian church, the fathers found in Stoicism arguments and an atmosphere of rationalism, monism, and optimism which combatted Gnosticism.

It was not primarily the 'materialism' of the Stoics, then, that Augustine was concerned to refute, but that of Manichaeism. It was the rejection of Manichaean materialism that committed him to an active theory of sensation. He wished to incorporate in his theory the most useful aspects of the Stoic theory. The

Stoic doctrine of πνεῦμα was introduced to account for sensation in a manner which Augustine would not have found inconsistent with the Neoplatonic spiritualistic account. But the problem remains, and Augustine was aware of it: a monistic account of sensation can never explain how the 'gap' between a spiritual soul and a material body can be bridged. If modifications in the body require the presence of a sense object to effect them, then the soul's act of sensing is dependent not only on the body's modifications, but also on the object of sense, a "detestable belief."[42] The discussion in De musica VI ends in the master's affirmation of the absolute transcendence of soul over body, requiring the nonpermeability of soul by the modifications of body; but apparently Augustine himself was not satisfied with the outcome, for he concludes:

> But if, because of the infirmity of either or both of us, the result should be less than we wish, either we ourselves shall investigate it at another time when we are less agitated, or we shall leave it to more intelligent people to examine, or, unworried, we shall leave it unsolved.[43]

Augustine's commentators agree with him in this feeling of dissatisfaction with the argument. Apparently the difficulty lies not in Augustine's insistence on the activity or the spirituality of the soul but in his failure to question the hierarchical structure which made it impossible for him to consider any action by body on soul. Yet, Robert E. Buckenmeyer has discussed several significant 'suggestions' in the Cassiciacum dialogues which require a different interpretation from Augustine's consciously formulated theory of sensation:

> First, the view that words are necessary instruments for the 'seekers' of learning within the De magistro suggest dependence of reason, the 'eye of the soul,' and basically, intelligence, the 'look of the soul,' upon the senses. Secondly, the statement that the senses are instruments of the soul's sensing in De quantitate animae implies that the soul has a conscious dependence on the body's 'passions.' Thirdly, the importance Augustine places upon writing down his so-called philosophical dialogues and the emphasis he puts on memory imply that both reason and intelligence need physical signs. Fourthly, . . . the comparison of the senses with a ship and of knowledge with a harbor in the Soliloquies require the

> <u>dependence of knowledge upon sense for the itinerant man</u>.[44]

Buckenmeyer concludes that, far from implying a pejorative view of the body's usefulness in the early dialogues, "Augustine implies a close, co-operative, what I would call a cumulative effect, between soul and body." Because of the way in which the soul is present to the body, not as one 'substance' either internal or external to another, but as intrinsic to and permeating the body, the primary intention of the soul is to attend to the body. Likewise, "the primary function of sensation is not to picture for the mind what things are like, but to warn the soul of changes in the body."[45] The movement of the soul in sensation is a breathing motion: that of "pouring itself back"--<u>refundere</u>[46]--into the animated body in the act of sensing, and then returning to itself, that is, "real-izing" the object of sense, systole and diastole. Thus "the soul's 'being moved' by the body is, after all, the result of its own initial act whereby the body is animated . . . the soul uses the body as an instrument to bring itself into contact with the sensible world of signs and similarities; thus it effects itself through the body."[47] To the question, does the soul learn through the body? then, Augustine answers that it does so in two ways: first, the soul can discover the order and beauty of the world and thus infer its Creator,[48] and secondly, the soul can order the "various sense perceptions of the world into academic disciplines and thus attain wisdom."[49]

But these possibilities of a mutual influence of soul and body, so ably described by Buckenmeyer, have a common characteristic: they occur in the early dialogues, not as conscious affirmations of the meaning and value of the body and its role in knowing and being, but as metaphors[50] or as casual, almost unguarded remarks in nonsystematic contexts. They reveal more than they intend to convey; they indicate an unconscious conflict between a formulated conceptual scheme in which, by definition, body can have no effect on soul because it is metaphysically inferior, and Augustine's intuition and experience of its value as an instrument of learning. Augustine was caught in this conflict by his concern to incorporate Plotinus' rejection of materialism and passivity in his theory of sensation, and by his attempt to synthesize the Stoic idea of πνεῦμα with Neoplatonic spiritualism.

Yet Augustine pressed this metaphysical hierarchy of values into a more extreme statement of the body's inability to act upon the soul than Plotinus himself. Had Augustine investigated Plotinus more systematically he would have found careful statements of the usefulness of sensation,[51] and even the acknowledgment of the possibility of "a sort of knowledge that is not without refinement, such as knowledge of the sun, the other planets, the heaven and the earth."[52] In addition, Plotinus found other positive values in sensation: "sensation provides contents for memory";[53] and "discursive reason passing judgments upon sense impressions already contemplates forms and contemplates them as it were with sensation."[54] Also, Plato's doctrine of reminiscences is understood by Plotinus to require sensation: ". . . understanding is gained as the soul recognizes and harmonizes the new and recently arrived impressions with those inherent in it of old. And this is what is meant by the soul's reminiscence."[55] Gordon Clark has demonstrated the "strict continuity" established by Plotinus "from sensation through memory and imagination on to discursion and at last even to intellect."[56]

> Sensation can imitate knowledge for the express reason that sensible objects are ideas extended in space. They are the visual, or sensible images of eternal realities; . . . man here is a being of sense because his perception is weaker and what he grasps are weak images of objects there. Consequently sensations here are obscure intellections and intellections there are clear sensations.[57]

Perhaps Augustine was confused, as are many modern interpreters of Plotinus, by the exhortation to leave the realm of sensation, to "fly the body." And Ambrose would have strongly reinforced this emphasis by constantly warning his hearers to "fly from temporal things and to ascend to the eternal and invisible,"[58] and to "shun the things of sense."[59] Yet the exhortation to go beyond the realm of sensation cannot be construed as implying a perjorative estimate of sensation or a retraction of Plotinus' theory of sensation, but a "confirmation" of it.[60] Plotinus is urging rather that we do not <u>conclude</u> our investigations of the world and the self at the level of sensation. He is putting sensation "in its place" and so guaranteeing its appropriate value as the basis of intellection, the necessary, but not sufficient, first step toward knowledge.[61] Sensation comes first; if one does not use the capacity of sensation with attention and precision, he will never come to knowledge: "For the intelligible object comes to us only when the soul has descended to the level of sensation."[62] The soul needs sense organs: "To grasp these sensible forms, the soul cannot be alone without an organ, for by itself it perceives its own content, and this is intellection, not sensation."[63] In itself, the pure soul has no means for grasping a sensible object, and we have seen that the soul begins its journey to intelligibles with sensation: "In literal sensation . . . we are actually in touch with reality; to be sure, we do not have a very firm grasp on it, but at least it is a contact."[64]

So Augustine, in the early dialogues, has, to some extent, outdone Plotinus in regarding sensation not only as last in the order of value, but as unable to initiate a motion toward knowledge. Sensation is certainly an activity for Augustine, and spiritual activity, but it is as if it were different in kind, in these early dialogues, from the higher spiritual activities. At this stage he confused sensations with the body since the objects of sense are bodies. He did this in spite of his insistence that sensation is not the body's work, but the soul's work. As bodies, the objects of sensation belong, in Augustine's and Plotinus' hierarchical universe, on the level of inferior beings, as distractions from intellection rather than aids to it. As bodies, sense objects participate strongly in matter, and this seriously distorts their truth value. Augustine was still, at this time, feeling the weight of his recent experience as a Manichaean, his inability to conceive of the real existence of anything but bodies, his bondage to the sensual. This personal experience colors the vehemence with which he describes the body's comparative valuelessness.[65]

Yet, as we have seen, Augustine has, even in the early dialogues, unconsciously compromised this explicit insistence on an active theory of sensation; an ambivalence emerges; bodies and sensation are important, so important, in fact, that the Augustine of the Cassiciacum dialogues must underplay their value. One example will suffice: in *De quantitate animae* 32, Augustine compares the meaning (*significatio*) communicated by a word and its sound (*sonus*) with the soul in relation to the body. As a rhetorician, Augustine was trained in the skill of using words which moved not only by their *significatio*, but also by their *sonus*. The analogy does not illuminate what Augustine intended to illuminate,[66] the worthlessness of *sonus* in comparison with *significatio*. At the time of the early dialogues, Augustine's unconscious metaphors betray his real ambivalence about the meaning and value of the body and a corresponding conscious emphasis on its worthlessness. In addition, his use of the Stoic concept of πνεῦμα, with all its connotations, indicates his discomfort with a conception of the hierarchical structure of human being which does not adequately account for the role of the body in sensation. His own conclusion of the discussion in *De musica* VI indicates that the ambivalence was not entirely unconscious but that Augustine, in his present state of knowledge and experience, despaired of resolving it.[67]

ii

Let us now begin to explore Augustine's theory of sensation as he describes it in the works of his maturity. The sources most relevant here are *De Trinitate* XI, written between c. A.D. 400 and 416-419,[68] and *De genesi ad litteram*, written almost contemporaneously with *De Trinitate*,[69] over a period of fifteen years, and published c. 416. In Augustine's account of sensation in his mature works, the emphasis has changed subtly but significantly. In place of the Cassiciacum emphasis on the soul's prerogative of spiritual activity in sensation, there is an emphasis on the unity of the human being; sensation is even cited as the proof of that unity; in place of his earlier emphasis on the spiritual nature of sensation, there is an emphasis on the reality of external objects of sense, and, finally, in place of his insistence on the hierarchical arrangement of the components of human being in which lower cannot act upon higher, Augustine emphasizes that the real difficulty with sensation is the *transitoriness* of its objects. For the hierarchical spatial model of the parts of human being of Plotinus, he substituted a temporal model; he is now thinking in terms of describing human being in process, itinerant through time. I will discuss Augustine's mature theory of sensation in terms of these three emphases: (a) unity of human being, (b) reality of sense objects, and (c) transitoriness of sense objects.

a. Augustine does not retract the statements of his earlier works on theory of sensation in his mature works; the active theory is reaffirmed.[70] Affirmed also is the incorporeal spiritual nature of the soul.[71] But the emphasis has changed: Augustine no longer needs to underline so strongly the exclusive role of the soul in sensation. I disagree with Gilson's statement that "Augustine does absolutely nothing to close the gap he has made between body and soul."[72] In his mature works Augustine struggles--as Plotinus had struggled--to close this gap; his development of the concept of spiritus (πνεῦμα) is one of the important devices he uses to "close the gap"; it is parallel to Plotinus' device of making the soul twofold, "one part being the agent strictly and the other, that nature which is the result of the soul's illuminating or animating the body."[73] Spiritus, as described in De genesi ad litteram XII, plays this role of mediator in Augustine's mature theory of sensation, enabling him to feel that he has brought closer together body and soul in the act of sensation and so to stress that unity. "In the early works no specific power is designated for the process of making images or of storing them. It is the soul which knows and forms images."[74] Although Clark's evaluation of Plotinus' attempt to close the gap is equally applicable to Augustine's attempt, yet Augustine's attempt to "halve the distances" indicates his adjustment of values. Of Plotinus' attempt, Clark writes:

> The disparity between soul and object is halved by the organ; the disparity between organ and object is halved by the visual ray; the disparity between organ and soul is halved by this nature; and so one is to leap across the Grand Canyon by jumping half the distance first.[75]

Yet the fact that both thinkers feel compelled to make this attempt is significant.

What, then, is the role of *spiritus* in sensation? It is important to remember that what Augustine is doing when he discusses the role of *spiritus* is describing what is the case, not attempting to account for what is the case; that is, it is a philosophical, not a religious, description. *Spiritus* is a part of the soul, inferior to *mens*, the properly intellectual part, a "receptive, conserving activity of the experience of the external world,"[76] a receptacle which both forms the images of corporeal things, that is, words and images which designate and recall the objects of sensation,[77] and retains these images; it is thus also the originator of dreams[78] and other visions which are the result of sickness or hallucination. *Spiritus*, a part of the incorporeal soul, is a mediator within the soul between the intellectual part and the sensitive part.[79]

A brief survey of the ways in which πνεῦμα was used by authors from classical Greece to Augustine's time indicates that Augustine's use of the term, "namely an existing reality totally distinct from material beings and often with the connotation of some relationship with God,"[80] was "revolutionary rather than evolutionary."[81] Influenced by Pauline uses of πνεῦμα, Augustine added connotations which further enriched the term, one of the most important of which is the function of *spiritus* in connecting the activity of sensation and the sensual object. The authors of classical Greece used πνεῦμα in the physical sense of 'wind' or 'breath.' The philosophers, from Aristotle to Plotinus, refined the use of πνεῦμα to a matter which was extremely tenuous and whose function was to mediate between God and the world, or between body and soul. In addition,

> The Manichaeans, the earliest influence in Augustine's intellectual development, were forced by their pantheistic dualism into a maze of contradictions; both God and man were spoken of as a 'spiritual substance,' a reality which was not spiritual or immaterial in the technical sense, but which was composed of extremely tenuous matter somehow having purely immaterial properties.[82]

Porphyry and Plotinus thought of πνεῦμα as a sort of tenuous material 'wrapper' for the soul which mediates between body and soul, and, for Plotinus, leaves the soul at death because it no longer has any function.[83]

The Scriptural meanings of πνεῦμα or _spiritus_, which indicate "the divine influence in human life and activity,"[84] are contradictory to the philosophical meanings, and emerge from the experience of an antithesis between flesh and spirit, an existential dualism, not a metaphysical description or philosophical analysis.[85] In Paul's usage, πνεῦμα is "the name given to the incorporeal part of human nature . . . [which] has been elevated to express the new nature of divine origin within the Christian,"[86] and stands always in contrast to σάρχ, which "has been adapted to designate the sinful state of human nature."[87]

Augustine summarizes, in several passages in his mature works, the uses of _spiritus_: _De Trinitate_ XIV.16.22; _De genesi ad litteram_ XII.7-8; _Sermo_ CXXVIII.9; _De anima et ejus origine_ IV.23.37. "All the meanings of _spiritus_ enumerated in these catalogs, with the exception of '_corpus futurum_ . . . _in resurrectione_,' which is taken directly from I Corinthians 15:44, are strictly philosophical, rather than theological or ascetical."[88] The tremendously wide range of meanings and contexts in which Augustine uses the term necessitates his careful distinction of the usage in a particular context from other ways that he and others have used it.

We have seen above how profoundly Plotinian is the impulse to account for sensation by positioning a series of intermediaries between soul and body. Porphyry had continued and extended this, and it has been pointed out by Solignac that Porphyry's notion of πνεῦματικηψυχη (_anima spiritalis_) is parallel to Augustine's _spiritus_ in designating an "inferior level of the soul, in which the soul places itself when it turns itself toward bodily realities or the images of these realities."[89] But it was the Scriptural usage of _spiritus_ above all that attracted Augustine with his interest in describing human being in its concrete historical dimension: the Pauline description of the radical disjunction between σάρξ and πνεῦμα answered to Augustine's experience and formulated for him the central problem of human being, a "moral conflict within the human soul, not an encounter between opposing substances.[90]

Spiritus uses its faculty of sensation by creating an immediate transition from coroporeal vision to spiritual vision and then to intellectual vision.[91]

> In a normal experience the object is seen by the eye, an image is produced in the *spiritus* and the intellect recognizes either the sign or its signification. Thus corporeal vision is ordered to spiritual and spiritual to intellectual, and a human experience is not complete without the three.[92]

In the early dialogues, Augustine describes the action of *spiritus* as *attentio*; in *De musica* VI his discussion of *attentio* "reproduces," according to Rohmer, the Stoic description, "principe d'un mouvement de tension intérieur à nos organes sensibles, la κίνησισ τονική."[93] But does *spiritus* act internally to the body as part of the organic function of the vegetative existence, or is it really a transcendent principle, at least theoretically distinguishable from the bodily functions? By *De genesi ad litteram*, Augustine had replaced his term 'attention' with 'intention,' an act of the will, a spiritual action.[94] It is the difference between saying, with the Epicureans and the Stoics, that knowledge is ultimately derivable from sensation, or saying with the Platonists that "the canons of truth, beauty, and goodness cannot be derived from sensation alone."[95]

The *intentio* of *spiritus* thus forms the link between the purely physical object of sensation and the purely spiritual activity of sensation. Its necessity, for Augustine, was precisely to account for the possibility of a unified activity. *De Trinitate* XI.9.16 discusses the inseparability *in fact* of the distinction Augustine has made in theory between the stages of sense experience:

> For there are two visions, one of perception, the other of thought. But in order that this vision of thought may be brought about, something similar to it is wrought for this purpose in the memory from the vision of perception, to which the eye of the mind may turn itself in thinking in the same way, as the glance of the eyes turns itself in perceiving to the body. . . . But the will appears everywhere only as the unifier, so to speak, of the parent and the offspring. And for this reason it cannot be called either the parent or the offspring, no matter from where it may proceed.[96]

In addition, the *intentio* of *spiritus* guarantees the identity of the subjective image of the sensible object and the form of the object itself so that we are unable to distinguish between them: "But we do not discern the form of the body which we see, and the form which arises from it in the sense of the one who sees, by the same sense, because the connection between them is so close that there is no room for distinguishing them."[97]

Whether a pneumatic intermediary appears in a materialistic or a spiritualistic tradition determines whether it has the function of holding soul and body *apart*, or the function of forming links which operate to bring soul and body together in a unity. The pneumatic intermediaries of materialistic traditions, beginning with Aristotle's ὄγανον πρῶτον, "originate in the preoccupation that the human soul must not be soiled by direct contact with matter; the soul does not act directly on the bodily organs, but is served by the pneumatic intermediary who governs the physical body."[98] The concern of materialists, since by definition nothing but body can act, and body's primary property is to act on body, is to safeguard the purity of the soul from the pollution of the body. Thus pneumatic intermediaries function to hold apart these two 'bodies.' The function of the pneumatic intermediary, on the other hand, in a spiritualist tradition is different, because the problem it answers is different; this problem is to explain how a spiritual soul can participate with a material body at all in the human composite. As an answer to this problem, the pneumatic intermediary serves to link or unite these two apparently incommensurable substances. The function of *nature* in Plotinus, because of its spiritual emphasis as a part of the soul, is basically to provide a link, to "halve the distance" between body and soul rather than to hold them apart. Plotinus is always concerned to relate, to form links between the various aspects of being, to show, in the first instance, the way of ascent to the One by discursively connecting each step of the ascent, and secondly, to infer the process of emanation by reversing the process of ascent. If there is an unbridgeable gulf somewhere in the process of emanation, the ascent is impossible; rather, even matter itself is merely the 'limit' of the emanation. In addition, "it is a universal law in the Plotinian system that the higher must give itself to the lower, and that the soul must impart itself to body in order to realize its own implicit powers."[99] Augustine's _spiritus_, like Plotinus' _nature_, relates, links, soul and body because the problem it seeks to answer is how body and soul can cooperate at all.

b. This consideration brings us to the second development of emphasis which I find in Augustine's mature writings on sensation: his insistence on the external reality of the sensual object. _Spiritus_ 'represents' and stores images of sensible things as it is confronted with sensory objects. This is a very slippery part of Augustine's account of sense experience; he intends both to safeguard the activity of the soul and to guarantee the objective existence of sensory objects. _Spiritus_ "under the stimulation of sensory objects" doubles the corporeal impression by picturing; without this necessary activity, the existence of the sensory object and the sensory organ are not sufficient to provoke sensation. Yet the object signals its presence and appearance to _spiritus_.[100] The representation of the object which _spiritus_ creates is produced "by the influence which exterior things exert on our sense organs."[101] Augustine, in his mature writings, does not separate the activity of sensing from the object--which even "acts" on the organ of sense to incite the activity of _spiritus_--and the creative act of the soul in sensing: "The external object is necessary to maintain the impression on the sense, but what is known and judged by the soul is an incorporeal representation of the impression."[102] _Spiritus_ makes the object exist for the human being, but the object has already an objective existence.[103]

Let us shelve, for the moment, the question of how Augustine accounts for his affirmation that the actually existing object is the same as the representation of _spiritus_ in order to look at Plotinus' treatment of the question.

For Plotinus, the objective reality of the object of sensation was guaranteed by his doctrine of universal sympathy.[104] The theory of sympathy, by which objects affect each other, not by any material medium of connection but by their resemblance to each other, is a direct refutation of the mechanistic accounts of sensation of the Stoics, the Epicureans, and Aristotle.[105] It presupposes that the universe is a living being, an organism: "The eyes, for example, produce a sympathetic reaction in the stomach without affecting the more closely situated teeth. Similarly, in the universe one object is the agent and another is its patient, not by any means of rigid connection, but by an action at a distance depending on resemblance between the two objects."[106] A medium would only obscure and distort and dilute the object passing through it to the organ of sense: "a medium would dull one's perception." It would also mean that it is the medium one actually sees, not the object; also "we see an object where it is, that is, at a distance from us, and not in the soul as an impression would be."[107] Plotinus asserts in two passages that "sensation knows only external objects."[108] Plotinus is concerned in this passage with describing how the soul can perceive through the body at all, and he proceeds by distinguishing the role of nature from that of the intellect: external sensory objects are necessary for sensation; "Intellect is not related to its objects as sensation is to the sensible objects which exist independently. It actually is the things it knows."[109]

This distinction was also an important one for Augustine in describing the reality of the sensory object: "One sees nothing with the eyes except bodies";[110] but the soul can "see within itself what it has not seen anywhere else." It is precisely this contrast with the bodily senses which serves to underline the emancipation of mens. Although Augustine is clearly a realist in insisting that sensible objects exist independently of their being perceived, he is concerned to hold this position together with his active principle of sensation in which the soul does not receive, but creates perceptions. The objective existence of the sensible object is never, to my knowledge, questioned by Augustine in his mature works.

Frederick Copleston has suggested that Augustine, in Soliloquia II.7., had entertained "a form of idealism remarkably similar to that of . . . George Berkeley,"[111] This would be an attractive argument for Augustine's development of thought concerning sensation, but under closer scrutiny it does not remain valid; in Soliloquia II.7, Augustine's presentation of the idealistic argument is presented clearly as hypothetical and tentative, and I think we may understand his discussion of *phantasia* and *phantasm* in *De musica* VI.11.32 to represent his early view of the reality of sensible things. This argument is repeated in *De Trinitate* IX.11.16: "When we speak of bodies by means of the bodily sense, there arises in our mind some likeness of them, which is a phantasm of the memory; for the bodies themselves are not all in the mind, when we think them, but only the likeness of these bodies."[112] Thus it is correct to speak not of the development of an idea, but a development of emphasis.

In fact, in *De Trinitate* VIII.6.9, the same 'Berkeleian' argument is used by Augustine to indicate the importance of sensory experience; we *see* bodies, and from this experience together with our experience of our own souls, we *infer* the existence of souls:

> For we recognize the movements of bodies also from their resemblance to ourselves, and from this fact we perceive that others live besides ourselves, since we also move our body in living, as we observe these bodies to be moved. For even when a living body is moved there is no way opened for our eyes to see the soul, a thing which cannot be seen with the eyes; but we notice that something is present within the bulk, such as is present in us, so that we are able to move our bulk in a similar way, and this is the life and the soul. . . . Therefore we know the soul of anyone at all from our own, and from our own we believe of him whom we do not know.[113]

Finally, the 'City of God' roundly condemns "doubt in the evidence of the senses as being madness; [it] trusts the evidence of the senses in every matter; for the mind employs the senses through the agency of the body, and anyone who supposes that they can never be trusted is woefully mistaken."[114]

c. The third development of emphasis in Augustine's mature writings on the theory of sensation has to do with a shift in his preoccupation with metaphysical questions concerning the parts and essence of human being to a description of our experience of process in time.[115]

"A definition of what man's metaphysical essence could have implied as belonging by right to his nature is not to be found in Augustine. The point of view he takes is always . . .

historical and purely factual."[116] The significance of this change cannot be overestimated; few persons in the course of their lives manage a pervasive and fundamental change of outlook of this dimension, involving a change of the models that lie beneath and inform consciousness. We need to see Augustine's mature and later writings in the light of this development from the metaphysical, from accounting for the human condition by referring it to its construction, to description of our journey through time. R. A. Markus, noticing this change in perspective in Augustine during the course of the 390s, has characterized it as a change from "the dominance of philosophy to a dominance of eschatology."[117] The importance of this change on Augustine's theory of sensation is that in the mature writings one finds far less emphasis on human being as hierarchical. Augustine's central interest is no longer to place the parts of human being on a graded scale from lowest to highest in order to show exactly where on this scale an activity such as sensation occurs and which parts of the human composite it uses. That this change from a spatial to a temporal model may represent an actual increment in consciousness expressed as a description of human being is suggested by the findings of the phenomenologist Eugene Minkowski: "the essence of being is not 'a feeling of being,' of existence, but a feeling of participation in the flowing onward, <u>necessarily expressed in terms of time</u>, and secondarily expressed in terms of space."[118] Thus, in Augustine's mature works, there is an emphasis on the transitoriness of sensation; Augustine's discussions of sense experience inevitably include discussions of the role of memory in sensation: the transitoriness of sensation requires that the soul gather and relate, at every instant of sensation, the sensation with its context. The model of sensation used is that of <u>hearing</u>, rather than vision, because hearing illustrates more clearly the temporal quality of sensation.

> If the mind has not already formed an image of its perception through the ears, and has not retained it in memory, it will not know that the second syllable is really the second, since the first no longer exists--it vanished as soon as it struck the ear. Thus all conversation, all sweet song, in short, all bodily movement which accompanies our acts, is dissipated and perishes, and no

> progress would be possible if the mind did not retain the memory of past movements in order to link them to the ones following during the whole length of the action. Now the mind would not retain the memory of these movements if it did not form an image of them in itself.[119]

"No writer before Augustine has placed such stress on the transitory nature of sense experience; not even a single syllable could be grasped if its integrity were not guaranteed by the retention of each succeeding image in memory."[120]

R. A. Markus illuminates this change in perspective when he describes the tension between classical and biblical elements in Augustine's thinking, "disguised only by the occasional coincidence of the vocabularies in which they are expressed."

> The imagery derived from the philosophical context is part of a cosmological scheme. The 'spiritual' is on a higher level than the 'carnal' in the cosmic order. Their relation can be pictured in spatial terms as 'above' and 'below.' The biblical opposition, on the other hand, depends on Christ's redemptive work: the 'spiritual' is what is transformed, the 'carnal' is unregenerated. The opposition is not between something cosmologically 'higher' and something 'lower.' It is one best expressed in temporal rather than spatial terms, as 'new' and 'old.' Thus, though capable of being rendered in the same terms, the two sets of contrasts are in reality essentially disparate. But Augustine did pass from the cosmological dualities of Neoplatonism to the temporal dualities of biblical redemption history.[121]

It was the influence of Scripture that determined this shift of Augustine's focus from the spatial cosmology of the philosophers to biblical dualities of time and eternity.[122] The congruence of vocabularies, as Markus has shown, made it possible for this change to occur almost imperceptibly and over a long period of time, roughly during the 390s. Scriptural, especially Pauline, anthropology speaks of 'old' and 'new,' not 'higher' and 'lower,' self. In the writings of the mature Augustine, the difficulty with sensation is its transitoriness: not only are the objects of sensation transitory, but the sense organs themselves mutate: "Nobody hath the same from himself. Mark this brethren: the body that he hath is not the same, for it standeth not in itself. It is changed with each period of life; it is changed by change of place and time; it is changed through disease and wastings of the flesh. It standeth not therefore in itself."[123]

Yet Augustine's anthropology retains the spatial metaphor of Plotinus and the change is one of emphasis rather than concept. Augustine gave a new layer of richness to the spatial metaphors by bonding onto them the biblical imagery. Again, I do not think we have shifts of ideas, but subtle, yet significant, shifts of emphasis. Spatial metaphors are never retracted, but are rather strengthened and reinforced by biblical images and metaphors.[124]

The emphasis on the transitoriness of sensation in Augustine's mature works has as its focus precisely this shift in which sensation is given a low but fundamental place in the functions and powers of human being. It is the soul's confusion of the two radically different experiences of knowing which enslaves human beings to the sensible world. De Trinitate X.5.7 describes the process by which the soul, which is unified with the body by a natural and powerful affinity, or love, comes to find it impossible to distinguish itself and its proper objects from sensible corporeal objects: "because it is in those things which it thinks of lovingly, and is lovingly habituated to the sensible, that is corporeal things, it is unable to be in itself without the images of those sensible things. Hence shameful error arises to block the way, whilst it has not the power to separate itself from the images of sensible things, so as to see itself alone. For they have marvelously cohered with it through the strong bond of love."[125] It is the inevitable association of corporeal objects with transitoriness which renders them untrustworthy for permanent knowledge, and it is easy to confuse these very different approaches to the value of bodies. We may here be making a distinction which Augustine himself never clarified; he writes at all periods as if he thinks that sensible objects are untrustworthy both because of their absolute subordination to noncorporeal entities,[126] and because the knowledge of transitory things is of such limited value toward knowing God and the self.

Another aspect of Augustine's preoccupation with transitoriness is relevant here. Peter Brown, in Augustine of Hippo, has masterfully described Augustine's change from imaging his life as that of a Platonic _sapiens_, living in increasingly perfected contemplation to that of a human being hampered and limited at every turn, not so much by the external world as by the force of memory which locks a person into habitual ways of action and response. Augustine writes in the _Confessions_:

> And sometimes working within me you open for me a door into a state of feeling which is quite unlike anything to which I am used--a kind of sweet delight which, if I could only remain permanently in that state, would be something not of this world, not of this life. But my sad weight makes me fall back again; I am swallowed up by normality (_resorbeor solitis_); I am held fast, and heavily do I weep, but heavily I am held. So much are we weighted down by the burden of custom![127]

This force of habit, this spiritual inertia, Augustine sees as caused by the identification of the soul with its experience with the transitory objects of sensation. He has come to an understanding of Paul's great antithesis of 'flesh' and 'spirit' along these lines:

> Previously he had interpreted Paul as a Platonist: he had seen him as the exponent of a spiritual ascent. . . . The idea of the spiritual life as a vertical ascent, as a progress towards a final, highest stage to be reached in this life, had fascinated Augustine in previous years. Now he will see in Paul nothing but a single, unresolved tension between 'flesh' and 'spirit.'[128]

This tension between 'flesh' and 'spirit' which became such a powerful formulation of man's existence for Augustine expresses an existential, psychological dualism, and in moving to this concrete historical model of human being, Augustine, like Paul, went beyond a philosophical or metaphysical definition. "St. Paul is discussing not man in general, nor man in the abstract, but man as he is, much in the same way in which Augustine will later consider the same subject."[129] This dichotomy between the spiritual and all phases of bodily existence which informs Augustine's anthropology is a contemporaneous development with his immersion in the theology of St. Paul; it is a dichotomy which has as its characteristic image in the mature Augustine that of a long journey along a 'darkening highway.'[130] It is no longer for Augustine a simple matter, however difficult in practice, of removing one's attention from the valueless objects of the life of sensation and of identification with eternal spiritual truth; the spiritual life itself is a process, intimately related to the processes of time, and weaving through time in brief flashes of vision and insight, but never, in this life, to be free of consuetudo carnalis, the danger of losing itself in sensation.

iii

The writings of Augustine's later years never deal directly with the operation and usefulness of sensation; Augustine does not reopen the subject for conceptual investigation or speculation. In his later writings, from approximately A.D. 418-420 on, he makes use of the scheme of sensation which the mature works define. Yet it is both interesting and important to explore the way in which Augustine came to render concrete and practical a theory of the value of sensation that had earlier in his life been abstract; it was Augustine's characteristic method to analyze a problem before he worked out its practical implications. His interest in miracles, not only new at this period but also in contradiction to his early view of the usefulness of the data of the senses, is perhaps the clearest indication of the change of perspective which we have been considering.

In De vera religione XXV.47 and De utilitate credendi 16.34, for example, Augustine had stated that miracles related specifically to a particular stage in Christianity and that their usefulness and therefore their occurrence was over:

> We have heard that our predecessors, at a stage in faith on the way from temporal things up to eternal things, followed visible miracles. They could do nothing else . . . miracles were not allowed to continue to our time, lest the mind should always seek visible things. . . . At that time the problem was to get people to believe before anyone was fit to reason about divine and invisible things.[131]

Clearly, for the young Augustine,[132] there was no place in his "harmonious rational universe" for the "marvelous, bizarre, and unexpected."[133] But the Retractationes correct this earlier assertion that miracles ceased after apostolic times.[134] The young Augustine had stressed that in present times, it was not the outer but the inner eyes that are opened because spiritual healing is more valuable than healing of the body. But he was speaking differently by the time he was forty-five, *circa* A.D. 400. After A.D. 415 he regards the answers to prayers at the *memoria* of martyrs as miracles.[135] It is too dramatic an about-face to have no connection with his changed emphasis on the unity of human being. "In the last years of Augustine's life, both sermons and writings are full of the stories of miracles."[136] Indeed, the grand finale of the *De civitate Dei* includes an almost tedious listing of miracles of his direct experience or trustworthy hearsay. His concern is precisely to verify and to make public current miracles. This passage, *De civitate Dei* XXII, written in approximately A.D. 425,[137] reads much more like the Bede of two centuries later than the Augustine of twenty years before.

How can we account for this reversal of Augustine's thought? We must be careful not to oversimplify; but I think that it is closely tied to a concretizing of his abstract theory of sensation, occasioned by historical as well as developmental factors. First, the flooding into the Christian Church of masses of people in the fourth and early fifth centuries may have prompted Augustine to think that the situation in which miracles were originally useful was being duplicated.[138] Secondly, Augustine experienced an increasing disenchantment with the results of the operation of reason alone. As Gilson has remarked in describing this change, Augustine discovered that it is "eminently reasonable not to rely on reason alone."[139] Thirdly, Augustine's increased and expanded awareness of the integration of human being and knowledge had directly to do with an altered evaluation of the body: for example, the function of miracles, Augustine wrote in *De civitate Dei* XXII.8, is intimately linked with the bodily resurrection of Christ: "many miracles have occurred, as we cannot deny, to testify to that one supreme miracle of salvation, the miracle of Christ's ascension into heaven in the flesh in which he rose from the dead."[140]

Miracles, especially the healing miracles which Augustine proceeds to enumerate, prove the bond between Christ's resurrection and the value of the body and the objects of sense: "What do these miracles attest but the faith which proclaims that Christ rose in the flesh and ascended into heaven with the flesh?"[141] His description of miracles in Book XXII leads directly, in chapters 10, 11, and 12, to arguing for the bodily resurrection. We will examine this argument more thoroughly in Chapter V; it is enough for now to recognize that, for Augustine, the bodily resurrection makes miracles possible.[142] And, in turn, the surest sign of the truth of the bodily resurrection is the visible miracles already apparent to us: both relate directly to the unity of the human being. Thus Augustine not only accepted but insisted on the publication of accounts of well-attested miracles.

> I have been concerned that such accounts should be published because I saw that signs of divine power like those of older days were frequently occurring in modern times too, and I felt that they should not pass into oblivion, unnoticed by people in general.[143]

There is a further aspect of Augustine's later interest in miracles which is relevant here, that is, the ubiquitousness of miracle as a measure of the habituation and sluggishness of the rational mind; the function of miracles is to startle human beings into awareness. For Augustine the difference between nature and miracle is simply the categorizing of experience by "reason alone."

> For even as that which the servants put into the water-pots was turned into wine by the doing of the Lord, so in like manner also is what the clouds pour forth changed into wine by the doing of the same Lord. But we do not wonder at the latter because it happens every year: it has lost its marvelousness by its constant recurrence. And yet it suggests a greater consideration than that which was done in the water-pots. . . . But since men, intent on a different matter, have lost the consideration of the works of God by which they should daily praise Him as the Creator, God has, as it were, reserved to Himself the doing of certain extraordinary actions, that by striking them with wonder, he might rouse men as from sleep to worship Him. A dead man has risen again; men marvel: so many are born daily, and none marvels.[144]

"A 'miracle' for Augustine was just such a reminder of the bounds imposed on the mind by habit."[145]

> . . . when such things happen in, as it were, a continuous stream of ever-flowing succession, passing from the hidden to the visible and from the visible to the hidden, by a regular and beaten track, then they are called natural; but when for the admonition of men they are intruded by an unusual form of change, they are called miracles.[146]

Miracles press on our senses from every side: "For who is there that considers the works of God, whereby this whole world is governed and regulated, who is not overwhelmed with miracles? If he considers the vigorous power of a single grain of any seed whatever, it is a mighty thing, it inspires him with awe."[147] Nature itself is the uninterrupted miracle. Nothing, Augustine says, prevents us from experiencing it as such except our failure to order our affections rightly and to use our senses.[148]

Miracles also dramatize the value of the body:

> To 'heal the eyes of the heart' remained the essence of religion, but Augustine had now made room also for the fate of the body. . . . A God whose generosity had scattered so much purely physical beauty on the earth could not neglect physical illness. . . . These miracles had sprouted from the desperation of men afflicted 'by more diseases than any book of medicine could hold.'[149]

The old Augustine has come to have a deep empathy for human suffering. The enumeration, in _De civitate Dei_ XXII.22, of the pains and torments of the human race does not omit to detail purely physical pains that "threaten the body from without": bad weather, wild animals, poisons, accidents, disease, thirst and hunger, and even nightmares and hallucinations.[150]

Thus we see that Augustine values miracles, in his later years, in three ways, all of which are related to the unity of human being: miracles demonstrate this unity in ways available to the senses; miracles illustrate the inadequacy of reason alone to grasp the fundamental truths of human existence, and, finally, miracles are a paradigm and earnest of the eventual redemption of the whole human being in the resurrection of the body. It is only in the context of Augustine's gradual development of thought concerning the role and value of sensation that we can understand his later preoccupation with miracles. Lacking this context, this interest appears as "a sudden and unprepared surrender to popular credulity."[151]

In conclusion, what emerges from this study of the development of Augustine's idea of the function of sensation is that it was a lifelong formulation, a movement from an early philosophical-intellectual emphasis which dictated an unconscious denigration of sensation as revealed in Augustine's metaphors in the early dialogues, to an increasing understanding and emphasis on sensation as a valuable means of <u>real</u>-izing the unity of human being.

> What is soundness of body? It is to be insensible to nothing. . . . Therefore, not to be devoid of sensation like a stone or a tree or a corpse, but to live in the body without being sensible of its weight--this is to be sound in body.[152]

CHAPTER III

THE DEVELOPMENT OF EMPHASIS IN AUGUSTINE'S TEACHINGS ON ASCETICISM FROM THE CASSICIACUM DIALOGUES TO THE MATURE WRITINGS AND THE PELAGIAN CONTROVERSY

i

It is time that an unprejudiced study of asceticism was done, a study which explores the functions, both to the individual and to the culture in which it arises, of ascetic practices. Perhaps an exploration of Augustine's teaching on asceticism could be a contribution toward such a general study. Popular prejudice against asceticism as well as language which perpetuates and reinforces this prejudice makes it difficult to formulate adequate understandings of asceticism. Part of the widespread pejorative attitude toward any form of asceticism comes from the failure or inability to distinguish between an enormously wide range of motivations, practices, and goals in asceticism. One finds even very respectably educated people generalizing all forms of asceticism into "masochism"--a problematic word at best--and finding it anti-life, neurotic, or perverse. The problem of language is well illustrated by James Hillman, in an excellent article, "The Language of Psychology and the Speech of the Soul."[1] Hillman describes Kraft-Ebing's derivation of the term "masochism" from the aberrations of Sacher-Masoch's fictitious characters, and the later extension of the term by Freud to include emotions, fantasies, and character attitudes. He discusses the misunderstanding of the phenomenon of the union of *eros* and suffering caused by the reduction of these components to "pleasure" and "pain"--"by reason's definition mutually exclusive." The paradox of masochism, which demonstrates the power of the psyche to transcend its so-called basics "*Lust/Unlust*," is neither formulated nor acknowledged by this term which "collapses passion into pornography." The difference between the *gloria passionis* and masochism is evident in this description by Bernard of Clairvaux:

> For he [the martyr] does not feel his own wounds when he contemplates those of Christ. The martyr stands rejoicing and triumphant, even though his body is torn to pieces. . . . And this is the fruit of love, not of insensibility. (Neque hoc facit stupor, sed amor.)[2]

"And this is the fruit of love, not of insensibility": this is the key to differentiating active, productive, transcendent suffering from ascetic--or even masochistic--practices which may appear externally identical, but which arise from a desperate longing to feel, from "insensibility." Colin Wilson, in _Origins of the Sexual Impulse_, has demonstrated that sexual criminals have very feeble sexual reactions, not strong ones. We must, I think, be willing to go to the trouble of differentiating the vast range of behavior and motivation that lies between 'passion' and 'insensibility' when we try to understand asceticism, rather than indulging our very questionable penchant for "absolute clarity of vision, for simplicity, for complete definition"[3] on the basis of external behavior. If, then, even the phenomenon we have learned to call 'masochism' displays ambiguity as soon as we get beyond the level of visible behavior, we may expect asceticism, the renunciation or sacrifice of certain pleasures or luxuries, to be equally difficult to understand from behavior alone.

Let us begin by eliminating "masochism" from our exploration of Augustine's teachings; Augustine was not attracted by sensational or abusive practices. He can understand and admire the ecstasy of the martyrs _in extremis_, but he does not seek a similar experience. In Augustine's writing there is none of the conscious developed imagery of the _gloria passionis_ which we find much later in Bernard of Clairvaux or even Bonaventure.[4] In fact, E. Auerbach has remarked that in Augustine's presentation of dramatic events there is "almost no trace of what is the primary preoccupation of Ammianus and other authors of the period, even including the Christians among them: the vivid sensory depiction of outward events, especially of the magical, the morbid, and the horrible."[5] Augustine's reticence is all the more marked since it occurs in a tradition of African patristic authors from the writer of the _Passio Perpetuae_ to Jerome's contemporary and lively interest in martyrdom.

Peter Brown discusses the "apparently sudden crystallization of an ideology of the martyrs" in the late second and early third centuries, the change from a passive "lamb to the slaughter" image to an active imagery of triumph over the devil through martyrdom. The amphitheater is seen as the location for a victorious struggle with the powers of evil.[6] Perpetua, in her vision before her martyrdom, saw only martyrs in Paradise.[7] The first Christian writer who "placed the ascetic ideal on the same level as that of the martyr,"[8] Clement of Alexandria, emphasized the Christian life rather than the ideal of martyrdom. The imagery of triumphant combat transferred rather easily from martyrdom to asceticism;[9] fourth-century asceticism must be seen in the context of a branching or proliferation of the earlier imagery of triumphant martyrdom. It arose from the need to reinterpret a normative and powerful Christian image. Asceticism, like martyrdom, is discontinuous with ordinary human effort, will, or courage; it is a gift of God: "For that which is beyond nature is from the Author of nature . . . virginity cannot be commanded, but must be wished for, for things which are above us are matters for prayer rather than under mastery."[10] Yet the ascetic ideal, so ably urged by Origen, only came into prominence in Africa and the West during the reign of Constantine. The transition of Christian energies from the focus on martyrdom to emphasis on asceticism is still attested in the seventh-century _Barlaam and Joasaph_: "Monasticism arose from men's desire to become martyrs in will, that they might not miss the glory of them who were made perfect by blood."[11] "With the ending of persecution the substitution of ascetic for martyr as the highest of the Christian's goals became complete."[12] But in Africa, a focus on the value of martyrdom continued through the fourth century, especially among Donatist Christians like Petilian of Constantine, who wrote at the end of the century to his clergy: "He ordained that we should undergo death for the faith, which each man should do for the communion of the Church. For Christianity makes progress by the deaths of its followers."[13] Still, the mood of the fourth century was steadily veering toward the ascetic ideal. The transition was officially formulated by Eusebius: "the 'prophetic' or 'philosophic' life, meaning that of the ascetic, was the 'true citizenship of heaven according to the gospel.'"[14]

Let us explore briefly several of the functions of asceticism. Psychologically and culturally, asceticism functions as a method of gathering and focusing energy in a society in which energy is scattered and squandered. It is the deliberate decision to claim one's psychic energy and choose the direction of its use. Late Roman thinkers had for centuries been conscious of the need to gather and direct psychic energy. Stoics, Neoplatonists, Manichaeans, and patristic authors agreed that the psyche is a partially closed energy system,[15] that energy which is occupied in one activity is not available for another, and that, since the soul creates out of its own substance the images of sensory objects with which it occupies itself,[16] the way to intensify and increase spiritual energy is to withdraw some of the energy usually spent in cathecting sensory objects. To the point here is J. D. Unwin's research based on Freudian theory:

> After investigating the cultural behavior of eighty uncivilized, and the best known civilized societies, Dr. Unwin found a direct relation between the limitation of sexual opportunity and advance in civilization, both being measured by carefully defined objective tests. In particular, he showed that sexual continence greatly increased the expansive energy of a society.[17]

We have been discussing the positive aspect of late classical asceticism; there is, I think, a more negative, but still culturally functional, aspect. E. R. Dodds, discussing asceticism of this period, quotes Marcus Aurelius: "'It is hard for a man to endure himself.'" Men, he says, "were enabled to endure themselves by making a sharp dichotomy between the self and the body, and diverting their resentment onto the latter."[18] The question is one of attempting to see what are the tacitly accepted ways of venting frustration in a culture. Perhaps body-hatred in late Roman culture had the same function of focusing and venting frustration that neurosis has in ours. The underlying question, though, is why a culture opts for a particular form of expression of frustration. It is not, of course, a 'choice' in the sense of deliberation and conscious option, but the unanimity of late Roman sources that the body is the right place to focus one's frustrations indicates an implicit and unconscious cultural agreement which emerges, in the most careful and systematic thinkers of the period, as ambivalence about the body, and in writers of lesser stature, as unmitigated pejorative regard. Whether an author of our period is a responsible thinker or not has far more to do with the sort of statement he will make concerning the body than whether he is pagan or Christian, Neoplatonist or Gnostic.

To recapitulate: the positive motivation for ascetic living is sublimation, a transmutation of the tremendous primal energy of the will to live--of which the clearest expression is sexuality. The longing to have the same degree and intensity of energy on the spiritual level is the precise opposite of the negative form of asceticism which, without the activating force of spiritual imagination, manages only repression, the denial of the physical or sexual needs. Indeed, much of the asceticism of our period smacks strongly of repression--and of that which inevitably accompanies it--fantasy, an exaggerated and problematic fantasy life, the escalation of archetypal images of danger and delight. The _Vita S. Antonii_ of Athanasius illustrates such an approach to asceticism: the repression which causes a man "to blush every time he had to eat or satisfy any other bodily function,"[19] the fantasies of devils, beasts, and women threatening the fragile psychic equilibrium--all testify to the enervating activity of repression, the blockage in the flow of psychic energy which is the opposite motion from the sublimation of sexual energy.[20] Asceticism can be a manifestation of either the positive desire to garner and concentrate energy, or of the need to express frustration, or it can be a bewildering and complex mixture of both. Since external forms of asceticism do not provide a reliable gauge of motivation, the range of motivations and forms of 'hatred of the body' fills a continuum which is hardly acknowledged by the term itself.

The philosophic basis for hatred of the body seems to be the idea which goes back to Heraclitus and Empedocles that this life is the death--or deep sleep--of the soul. But, as Dodds remarks, "in our period it is associated with a new intensity of feeling. The body is the 'dark gaol, the living death, the corpse revealed, the tomb that we carry about with us.'"[21] This idea, a commonplace of ancient thought, was so pervasive that Christian authors, who might have recognized the need to restructure their thinking about the body because of the doctrines of creation, Incarnation, and the bodily resurrection, used these incongruent and inconsistent notions side by side with Christian ideas. Tertullian, for example, in De Anima 53, "after quoting St. Paul's description of the body as 'the temple of God,' . . . immediately goes on to say that it obstructs, obscures, and sullies the soul."[22]

There is no specific treatment of asceticism in Augustine's early dialogues, or until after his consecration as a bishop, but a point of view is assumed and implied. Let us first investigate the assumptions which provide the setting for this point of view. First, as discussed above, the body is always treated in the context of a comparison with the soul. The dialectical polarities, soul-body, immortal-mortal, rational-irrational, are rhetorical antitheses; they are employed not entirely as metaphysical entities, but as models of man's psychological structure. I agree with Fr. O'Connell's estimate of Augustine's anthropology that "'the Soul is the man,' the authentic 'I,'"[23] a view which repeats Plotinus' view, stated in Ennead IV.7.1: the body is "an instrument of ours . . . put at our service for a certain time," while the soul is "'the sovran principle, the authentic man' . . . whatever that relation be, the Soul is the man."

Yet Plotinus himself, on occasion, corrects the inadequacy of this formula,[24] and Augustine's interest in the soul in the early writings was not, as he was careful to spell out in De Moribus Ecclesiae Catholicae, a denunciation of the life of the body. Rather:

> If we seek what is best for the body, determined reason forces us to say: it is whatever makes the body to be at its best. But of all things that enliven the body, none are better or more primary than the soul. Thus, the highest good of the body is not its desires, nor absence of pain, nor its strength, nor its beauty, nor its speed, nor whatever else is counted among its goods, but, indeed, the soul. For the very

> presence of the soul offers the body all the things that were mentioned as well as that which excels them all, namely, life.[25]

Thus, the good of the body is integrated into any discussion of the good of the soul. This principle governs Augustine's conscious view of asceticism from his earliest statements.

Early Stoic theory also posits the unity and order of human being and stands in opposition to the Gnostics who made cosmological and psychological distinctions between the intelligible world and the sensible world, basing their teachings on asceticism on this distinction.[26] Yet, when we compare the metaphysical and the ethical statements of both the Stoics and the Platonists, a curious disjunction emerges. The Stoics' definition of 'body' as the only existent entity[27] asserts that "matter and the active shaping principle never exist apart from one another. Together they constitute all that exists, and they can only be drawn apart for the purpose of conceptual analysis."[28] But the ethics of the Stoics, probably formed with the Cynic influence of Diogenes and Antisthenes,[29] gave the fundamental Stoic notion that "the real nature of φύσις of a man consists in his rationality, . . . a particularly extreme and rigorous interpretation, an ascetic twist."[30] In the later Stoics the place of the body in bonding together logos and matter is honored in theory more than it is in practical ethics. Zeno and Chrysippus had explicitly denied that moral action is the result of a struggle between various elements of the personality; early Stoic philosophy had insisted on the psychosomatic nature of human being.[31] But the later Stoics regarded the body not as merely neutral, but as actively threatening the tranquility of the personality; Seneca writes: "Contempt for one's body is a sure sign of freedom. You can open the road to freedom with a lancet, and give tranquility at the price of a pin-prick."[32] The transition from regarding human being as irreducibly unitary, except for purposes of conceptual analysis, seems to have emerged with Panaetius, who contrasted the soul and nature while his predecessors had integrated them. This emphasis was continued and deepened in Posidonius. The assertion, common to Stoics and Epicureans, "that the wise and good man would be ευδαίμων on the rack or while being roasted alive in the brazen bull of Phalaris,"[33] implies radical ignoring of bodily reality.

Yet Stoic influence on Augustine, as on the earlier fathers, was in the direction of affirming the essential unity of the human composite and its larger unity with the cosmos. Spanneut finds, in fact, that one of the reasons that the Church fathers found the world view and many of the arguments of the Stoic philosophers useful and attractive in explicating Christian thought was their concern to combat Gnosticism, which they associated with Platonism; "they combatted dualism between God and man, body, and soul, and within the soul in its different modes of knowledge."[34] But the ambivalence, especially marked in the later Stoics, is also part of Augustine's heritage. We need also to make a distinction between systematic Stoic theory, available only to educated men, and the inevitable distortion of Stoic ideas in the process, centuries old by Augustine's time, of popularization of Stoic thought, a popularization which had sharpened the disjunction between early Stoic theory and later Stoic ethical emphasis. Certainly, Augustine was very attracted to the Stoic recommendation to continence which he read in the Hortensius at precisely the time which Baguette has argued was a Stoic period in his development.[35] "It certainly seems that the _Hortensius_ inspired a desire for continence in Augustine: such an aspiration appears to be attested from the period of this reading."[36] In summary, the effect of Stoic influence on Augustine must have been to impress him with its ambivalence concerning the value of bodily experience.

A similar ambivalence appears in Neoplatonism. A strong dualistic element appears in Middle Platonism in the thought of Numenius, who regarded embodiment as "always an evil for the soul."[37] The popular account of the soul's descent to this world, common to late Stoics and Platonists, imaged the soul as falling through the planetary spheres and in so doing acquiring increments of impurity.[38] The Neoplatonists rejected Numenius' formulation of matter as independent of God and identified with absolute evil, but Plotinus retained a modified view of the terrestrial body which was based on this fall of the soul into embodiment:

> . . . it is only when she reaches the terrestrial body shaped for her by the World-soul that her fall becomes complete.

> For now a new danger arises. In contrast to the all-inclusive body of the world and the subtle bodies of the stars, the human body is a complex and unstable combination of elements, needing perpetual replenishment and subject to external dangers. (IV.8.2.614) It is this instability which is the source of the desires and disturbances of man's lower nature and which necessitates deliberate intervention by his higher soul. . . . The human soul faces the danger that she may come to make care for the body and her lower nature her primary aim and so forget the Intelligible world.[39]

This is the potential danger of the soul's close association with a body, the danger that body and soul will become mixed, indistinguishable. This is an old theme in philosophy: Aristotle formulated it systematically in the *Nichomachean Ethics*: process of mind and process of body are distinguishable theoretically and must be distinguished practically if human beings are to actualize their potential for creative thought. Pétrement describes this danger of real loss of human potential due to failure to distinguish bodily and intellectual capacities: the firm resolution to be master of oneself "regards body passions as *movements of a machine*"; weakness, willingness not to choose is always based on the belief that the instincts of the body are "an obscure kind of thought, but deep and wise," so that "one shouldn't combat them."[40]

Yet Plotinus, having seen and stated the danger of being in a body, was then free to affirm Plato's suggestions in the *Timaeus* and the *Parmenides* that the sensible world is a good and beautiful image of the Intelligible. A. H. Armstrong has described the curious ambiguity of Plotinus' view of the sensible world and the "variations in its valuation" which emerge from it:

> All the reality which the image has is derived from its participation in its archetype. In so far as the image *is* anything at all it is what its archetype is. A 'slide' in estimation of the image is therefore possible. It may be thought of as having very little share in reality. . . . Or it may be seen as participating so fully in and being so close to its archetype that the archetype comes to be thought of as our living sense world in all its diversity 'seen from the inside.'[41]

Perhaps this begins to explain the enormous and complex range in Neoplatonic thought between Porphyry's remark that Plotinus "seemed ashamed of being in the body,"[42] and Plotinus' objections to the Gnostic complaints against the body.[43] No one, says Plotinus, who does not love its sensible offspring can truly love the Intelligible world.[44] Plotinus thus takes a very mild view of asceticism which we must see in the context of the thought of his time: "That sexual relations have value only for procreation had been implicit in Plato and was common ground for most moralists of late Antiquity. And the Symposium's doctrine that sexual energy is more profitably directed towards the Ideal world provided a strong incentive to total celibacy."[45] Plotinus did not marry, but his followers included married men and women; according to Porphyry, he was a vegetarian, but he does not mention this in the Enneads. He allowed, with Aristotle, that a moderate amount of external goods contributed to the happiness of the philosopher,[46] but an excess of them is a hindrance.[47] The main factor requiring asceticism is the danger of too much attention being directed toward the body.[48] Although, for Plotinus, the higher soul cannot be distracted from its contemplation of the One, yet the middle soul can incline to identification with the higher or the lower self of human beings. If the identification is with the latter, one "forgets" his/her true existence, which is true happiness. Therefore the body is to be disciplined in order to loosen its demand on the soul's attention, even to the extent, in some unusual circumstances, of sickness.[49] Yet normally the philosopher will preserve the health of the body,[50] and even though "the need to care for a body at all is a regrettable distraction,"[51] this distraction is not sufficient seriously to undermine the philosopher's true task. "Unlike the Gnostics, therefore, the Platonic sage will not revile the body; he will rather patiently await his release by death, when he will abandon it as a musician finally abandons a lyre that has served him well."[52] As for the popular Stoic and Epicurean notion that the sage ought to be perfectly happy while being roasted alive in the bull of Phalaris, Plotinus remarks, in I.4.13, that it is simply silly, even though, he adds, his philosophy would do a better job of accounting for this conceptually than Stoic philosophy.

The Stoics make no distinction in the components of human being between the part that is in torture and the part which remains in undisturbed contemplation, while Plotinus does distinguish: ". . . that which suffers pain is one thing, and there is another which, even while it is compelled to accompany that which suffers pain, remains in its own company and will not fall short of the vision of the universal good."[53]

Plotinus' thought concerning asceticism, then, is clearly formulated in Ennead I.4.14:

> He [the wise man] will take care of his bodily health, but will not wish to be altogether without experience of bodily illness, nor indeed also of pain. Rather, even if these do not come to him he will want to learn them while he is young, but when he is old he will not want either pains or pleasures to hinder him, or any earthly thing, pleasant or the reverse, so that he may not have to consider the body.[54]

The point seems to be integration of the variety and range of bodily experience into the life of the soul. The metaphor of the lyre is very apposite to Plotinus' careful description in I.4.16 of the productive way to regard the body:

> . . . some of his activities will tend towards well-being;[55] others will not be directed to the goal and will really not belong to him but to that which is joined to him (the body), which he will care for and bear with as long as he can, like a musician with his lyre, as long as he can use it; if he cannot use it, he will change to another, or give up using the lyre and abandon the activities directed to it. Then he will have something else to do and does not need the lyre, and will let it lie unregarded beside him while he sings without his instrument. Yet the instrument was not given him at the beginning without good reason. He has used it often up till now.

Although Plotinus reflects and transmits the ambivalence of Platonists from Plato forward concerning the meaning and value of the body, he has worked out a practical attitude toward ascetic practice which does not do violence to either pole of the ambiguity.

A final influence we must consider on Augustine's early view of asceticism is what Fr. O'Connell has termed an "unresolved Manichaean suspicion of the body."[56] The dialogues were written between November A.D. 386 and sometime in 389, the first of them only four years after Augustine's disillusionment with the Manichaeans;[57] although there is no specific treatment of asceticism in their pages, the emphasis on "flight from the body" can be found "on virtually every page" of these dialogues.[58] This is not a tendency to conceptual Manichaeism, but Augustine never ceased to experience the world dualistically, that is, as a struggle against the tremendous capacity of sensory objects for distraction.

Augustine's motivation for becoming a Manichee had been intellectual; he describes in the Confessions his pressing anxiety to have an explanation of the world which articulated his experience.[59] Augustine's frustration, which he describes as continuing throughout the Manichaean period,[60] was that in Manichaeism "even though emotional experience is expressed in the form of intellectual problems, these problems receive purely mythical solutions."[61] "These long fables of the Manichaeans," Augustine calls them.[62] Puech has aptly described the Manichaean quest:

> To the extent that his [the Gnostic's] temporal existence is unacceptable to his feeling, it shocks his reason. The emotional need for salvation raises intellectual problems. . . . The experience of evil is formulated on the plane of knowledge and demands explanation and solution on that plane.[63]

We need to balance very carefully Augustine's psychological predilection for dualism, an affinity which he shares with his fellow North Africans,[64] with his conscious correction of Manichaean ideas. It took Augustine some time to be able to articulate his confusion as a Manichee. The basis of a remark such as we find in Contra Academicos I.3: "We ought to have no concern for anything that can be discerned by mortal eyes or reached by any of the senses, but rather that all such things are to be disregarded," is illuminated accurately only by his later statement in De duabus animabus contra Manichaeos,[65] "I was not able at that time to distinguish and discern sensible from intelligible things, carnal from spiritual." It is wrong, as Augustine saw even by the time of the writing of the dialogues, to derive or deduce spiritual notions from visible objects. But it was only later that he could articulate this insight, which, at the writing of the dialogues, simply took the form of a denigration of sensory experience.

Had Augustine retained "exaggerated notions of standards of chastity" from his Manichaean[66] period? The question of why Augustine's conversion to Christianity took the form of a conversion to continence is an exceedingly complex one, but I think we must understand it partly as a movement toward integration of the driven compulsive sexuality of his youth which had been dissociated from his intellectual love of beauty and order. The degree of sensuality of Augustine's youth, a titillating question to more than historians, should be neither under-[67] nor overestimated; we would still not know how to interpret its significance even if we had all the information about it without a fact of fundamental importance: that is, that Augustine felt himself to be encapsulated, unfree in his sexuality, that it dominated and dictated; sexuality was the one area of Augustine's early life that escaped rational control. We do not need Augustine's Manichaeism, an intellectual quest that failed, to account for his conversion to continence.

Nor can Augustine's conversion be identified with the commonplace "conversions to philosophy" of his time.[68] Although this interpretation is tempting and would help us to understand Augustine's conversion to continence, since Augustine had found in Cicero's Hortensius an invitation to such philosophic continence,[69] it oversimplifies and externalizes what was essentially complex and subjective. Augustine had already rejected Alypius' argument for the necessity of continence for leading a philosophic life.[70] The specifically Christian character of Augustine's conversion to continence is attested by two consistent emphases: continence is a gift of God,[71] and it is not--emphatically not--a requirement for leading a Christian life; with St. Paul, "Augustine considered the life of continence as something 'better.'"[72]

Yet we need not deny that both unconscious Manichaean predilection, "in the air" in Augustine's North Africa, and the tradition of philosophic withdrawal to continence played minor roles in Augustine's decision to become continent. Also, I think that a healthy respect for what Jung has termed "the stability of the neuroses" was a major motivation of Augustine.

He was keenly and humbly aware that anyone who has been compulsive in an area can readily become so again; he recognized sexuality as beyond his capacity to integrate. Augustine knew himself to be a man of strong sensuality; he confesses his continual battle to be moderate in things which are impossible to give up "once and for all and never touch again, as I was able to do with sex."[73] We may recognize the principle as that of Alcoholics Anonymous and Synanon: there are persons for whom the only alternative to addiction is total abstinence.

In *De moribus Ecclesiae catholicae* and *Manichaeorum*,[74] Augustine's tone is different; since he is now dealing with a specifically religious topic, the perspective is altered from the philosophic ascetic tone of the dialogues to a specifically religious perspective. We find for the first time Augustine's characteristic and continuing emphasis on the body and bodily practices as significant only because of their effect on the soul: ". . . when we ask what kind of a life we must lead in order to attain happiness--the commandments are not for the body, and we are not concerned with bodily discipline."[75] Augustine's often-quoted definition of human being appears in this context: "Man as he appears to us is a rational soul making use of a mortal body."[76] In his discussion of different forms of dietary abstinence, for example, the ideal Augustine presents is one of simplicity or nonchalance, rather than of severe abstinence.[77] That which is of the first importance is a matter of the soul:[78] "Charity is safeguarded above all. It rules their eating, their speech, their dress, their countenance." As early as A.D. 390, in *De vera religione*, the emphasis is established: "It is easy to execrate the flesh, but very difficult not to be carnally minded."[79]

ii

We have now to look at the mature Augustine's views on asceticism. Preliminary to understanding these, however, we will need to discuss briefly the major influences on them, namely, Scripture and the earlier patristic writers.

J. A. T. Robinson has discussed the background in Hebrew thought for Paul's use of what Robinson calls an "uncompromisingly physical" understanding of the Church as the "Body of

Christ."[80] Old Testament thought, in contrast to Greek thought which distinguishes between form and matter, the whole and its parts, and body and soul, employs only one word, basar, to designate "the whole life-substance of men or beasts as organized in corporeal form . . . and the powers and the functions of the personality are regarded as exercised through a great variety of organs, indifferently physical and psychical."[81] This Hebrew emphasis on the whole human being, this unwillingness to abstract beyond experience, not a specifically philosophic position,[82] informed Paul's use of "Body of Christ" to designate the Church: "It is almost impossible to exaggerate the materialism and crudity of Paul's doctrine of the Church as literally now the resurrection body of Christ."[83]

> . . . the fact that it is a spiritual body does not mean that it is not physical. To such an extent is the new union with Christ physical (the word 'joined' is again one of sexual union--καλλᾶσθαι) that immoral sex relations can destroy it. It is in their bodies (I Cor. VI.15)--as σώματα and not merely as 'spirits' --that Christians are members of Christ.[84]

This is the Scriptural--specifically the Pauline--basis for asceticism: the bodily activities, especially sexual activities, are no longer a matter of indifference; "the sexual is a way the soul speaks."[85] In the Christian commitment there is "an immediate transition from the body as the carrier of sex to the body as a man's very self."[86] The body is quite literally included in salvation; the Christian can no longer avoid the difficult task of integrating his/her sexuality. Here is a positive rationale, based not on a denigration of the body but on the assumption of its essential goodness as created, and the necessity of bonding its activities within the whole human being. Paul's preoccupation with this struggle, for which he employs the strongest metaphors--a war or a race--tends to obscure the fact that the struggle to integrate is not against an enemy, but rather the struggle is necessary because of the tremendous lif-energy contained by the body, an energy which must be retained and made available to the spirit. For Augustine the difficulty of so integrating the notoriously recalcitrant body is the only reason for any practice of asceticism.[87]

The second major influence on Augustine's mature teachings on asceticism, that of the earlier patristic authors, must be discussed under two general headings, the Alexandrian view, as represented by Clement and Origen, and the Western view as represented by Tertullian and Cyprian. Frend discusses the emergence of this distinction as a direct result of the gradual substitution in the East of a metaphysical for an apocalyptic view of Christianity,[88] while the apocalyptic emphasis in Rome and North Africa was continued and intensified by Tertullian, Montanism, and eventually Donatism. The "first explicit statement of two contrasting views of martyrdom" occurs in Clement of Alexandria's Stromata IV.4.17-18. Clement emphasized the "martyrdom of everyday life, of word, life, conduct, of the whole man."[89]

Other emphases related to asceticism differentiated East from West in the third and fourth centuries. The apocalyptic orientation of the West resulted in an emphasis on martyrdom which was valued, more and more, for example, by Tertullian.[90] There was an attitude of puritanical nonconformism, denigration of classical learning, or, more pervasively, rejection of the model of gradual but steady learning as a description of the Christian life in favor of what Auerbach has termed the "characteristically Christian . . . about-face from one extreme to its very opposite";[91] in short, western Christians tended to experience the surrounding world as irreducibly hostile. Apocalyptic expectations were also at the roots of Tertullian's teachings on marriage. In Ad Uxorem I, he concedes that marriage is needed to propagate the human race, but later, in De Exhortatione Castitatis, he instead emphasized the futility of propagation when the End is so imminent. Asceticism for the purpose of rendering the body a useful servant to the soul is seen only as an adjunct or preparation for martyrdom. The radical individualism of Tertullian's statement: "My only concern is for myself, careful for nothing except that I should have no care,"[92] also is a value dictated by the goal of martyrdom. Martyrdom is essentially a solitary act, motivated, not by deep social concern or love of family and friends, but by the individual consciousness in direct confrontation with God, the Judge. Cyprian, for whom Tertullian was 'the master,' likewise emphasized sin, separation from the world, sudden liberation through baptism, and the abandonment of previous interests.[93] This focus on martyrdom in the West cannot be explained on the basis of greater severity of persecution. Frend describes the effects of the A.D. 303-312 persecution in East and West:

> Altogether in the west, the persecution hardly deserves the title of 'Great.' Outside of the province of Numidia there were relatively few victims. Church life was disrupted and ecclesiastics discredited but the laity as a whole were little affected. Even before the abdication of Diocletian, persecution in North Africa was ending. Just as under Decius, the authorities seem to have been satisfied once the Imperial orders had been given formal obedience. . . . In the east there were to be six more years of misery. . . . (p. 505) In the east . . . one feels a deeper sense of urgency. The persecution was part of a long-drawn-out battle for the minds of the provincials, the final bloody act of a great tragedy.[94]

It is ironic that Tertullian, who had so valued and urged martyrdom, apparently died peacefully of old age; Origen, also a zealot for martyrdom, but "a founding influence on monasticism,"[95] died as the result of imprisonment and prolonged torture in the Decian persecution. The long life of the Christian ascetic, said Origen, "could be of equal importance [with martyrdom] as an expiation of sin,[96] or as an example to others."[97] He consistently emphasized the gradual growth of the Christian; bodily asceticism relates to the focusing of energy on appropriating the "higher image of God."[98] Like Clement, Origen viewed martyrdom as only one of the paths to remission of sins; he placed it second to baptism.[99]

> . . . not for nothing is Origen accounted as one of the founding influences in Egyptian monasticism. . . . His 'philosophical' way of life, as described by Eusebius, was that of an ascetic, frugal, without material comforts, sexless, free from all but the most necessary possessions, and we are told he encouraged 'thousands' to do likewise for their own progress towards enlightenment.[100]

In the fourth century, after the Constantinian settlement, both East and West began to emphasize asceticism. Laeuchli writes: "the whole ascetic and penitential life of the fourth century Christian Church was outside the trinitarian speculations, devoid of all these monistic tendencies."[101] It is interesting to note here the divergence between theoretical description and practice. The sharpening of monistic metaphysical descriptions occurred in the context of an intensified experiential dualism. The strong sexual dualism of late antiquity appears in penitential practice--"a gradual confusion of discipline with dualism," Laeuchli claims. I think it was rather that the fine minds of the time could distinguish between metaphysical description and experiential necessity; popular thought could not, and for popular thought, practice always precedes and determines theory. The exaggerated emphasis on sexual behavior was not uncontested; the Synod of Gangra, in the mid-fourth century,[102] "challenged not only the panic concerning sex, but ascetic irresponsibility and contempt for marriage."[103] The alarm caused by the followers of Eustathius, who held that "no married person has hope with God," and dissolved marriages, refusing to pray or to participate in the Eucharist in the homes of married persons, prompted the Synod of Gangra to pronounce anathema on anyone who "lives unmarried or in continence, avoiding marriage from contempt and not because of the beauty and holiness of virginity."[104] These abuses of asceticism are difficult to interpret; they might demonstrate either the intensification of a growing interest in asceticism, or a reaction to the increasing numbers of nominal Christians who poured into the fourth-century church and threatened to dilute beyond recognition its ethical requirements.

It is significant, however, that it was at Gangra, located on the outer circle of the Mediterranean that these practices were censured.[105] In the center of the circle, Rome, "the history of the conversion of Roman families is part of the history of an extreme 'oriental' form of asceticism on the religious life of Rome.'[106] Ambrose, the author of the first manual of Christian ethics, *De officiis ministrorum*, exhibits ambivalence about the value of the body which takes the form of creating an apparent contradiction between theory and practice. The body, although for Ambrose a "superb work of divine art," differs from the soul in substance, nature, and tendency, so that "what is according to the nature of the body is contrary to the nature of the soul."[107] Yet this distinction of body and soul does not give a basis for Ambrose's disparaging remarks about the body: ". . . for it is not possible to be at home with God and with the flesh at the same time."[108] He goes beyond Stoic philosophers in asserting that not only is death not an evil, but it is a positive good: "Thus, while the Stoic shows only contempt of death, the Christian exhibits love of death."[109] In Ambrose, the ascetic emphasis of the East and the emphasis on martyrdom of the West come together in a way that strongly influenced Augustine. Ambrose inherited what Dudden calls a "gloomy view of the world" derived from Philo, and the ascetic teachings of the Cappadocians,[110] especially Basil's teaching that "the demands and even the existence of the body [should] be acknowledged only when necessary."[111] Peter Brown writes of "two Ambroses," the great missionary bishop, and "the ascete, the man with a sensitive revulsion for the human condition, 'swaddled in passion'; the Platonist for whom any earthly perfection is vanity."[112] Ambrose preached a Porphyrian asceticism, especially in the sermon on the Hexameron, which Augustine heard on 4 April 386.[113] Porphyry's asceticism was "certainly more crudely otherworldly and dualistic" than that of Plotinus, and "seems to have preached 'flight from the body' without the nuances, qualifications, and suggestions of a quite different attitude which can sometimes be discovered in Plotinus."[114]

It is in the light of Ambrose's "preference for practical problems"[115] that we may interpret his emphasis on asceticism. The experiential need to order the needs and passions of the body was of more pressing interest to him than metaphysical description. We can understand, then, his predilection for generalizing his theology of original sin, for example, from the experience of body-soul dualism. He posited a *physical* basis for original sin,[116] even though he asserted the spirituality of the soul; but "unless soul is body, as Tertullian thought, or a function of body, conditions of physical propagation can never explain a spiritual fact."[117] In all, the influence of Ambrose on Augustine was a skillful amalgam of Stoic, Neoplatonic, and Christian asceticism. In his treatise *De virginitate*, Ambrose demonstrates the lack of fanaticism in his exhortation to virginity; he repeats that virginity is a *gift* of God[118] and calls marriage also a "gift":

> Some one may say, 'Do you, then, discourage marriage?' Nay, I encourage it, and condemn those who are wont to discourage it. . . . For he who condemns marriage, condemns the birth of children and condemns the fellowship of the human race, continued by a series of successive generations--for how can generation succeed generation in a continual order, unless the gift of marriage stirred up a desire for offspring.[119]

We will see how this emphasis on asceticism, held together with respect for the variety of 'gifts' which determine the optimal productivity of different persons, is continued and intensified in Augustine's mature teachings on asceticism.

In summary, the influence of earlier and contemporary patristic authors on Augustine had the effect of making him assume the usefulness of some form of bodily discipline beyond that of the 'letter of the law' for consolidating and directing psychic energy toward spiritual growth. Let us now consider four ascetical treatises of Augustine's maturity: *De utilitate jejunii*, A.D. 408-412; *De bono coniungali*, A.D. 401; *De sancta virginitate*, A.D. 401; and *De continentia*, A.D. 414-416.[120] These are the works in which the body is the *theme*, in which we may expect a different emphasis from works in which the body is treated as a foil to demonstrate the greatness of the soul.

Let us look first at *De continentia*; we will look for Augustine's emphasis by following his argument. He first designates the kind of continence which he is treating as specifically Christian continence: continence is "a gift of God . . . unless God give it, it is possible for no one to be continent."[121] He then quotes I Corinthians 7.7: "For I would that all men were as myself, but each one has his own gift from God, one in this way and another in that." Secondly, continence refers not only to the lust of the flesh, but more significantly to the disposition of the heart; "there are many things which we do not speak from the mouth of the body, but shout from the heart."[122] Thus it is a matter of first cleaning "what things are inside." This thought leads Augustine directly to dealing with the nature of the flesh. It is significant that in this treatise on continence, about half the length of it is devoted to defending the flesh! Continence is, if anything, slightly denigrated as a negative virtue: "continence is necessary for us in order to turn away from evil. But that we do good seems to pertain to another virtue, namely justice."[123]

Augustine reminds us that our flesh is both good and 'natural': "medicinal aid is sought from Him who can heal all languors . . . not in the separation of an alien nature from us, but in the repair of our own nature."[124] The reason that the soul should rule the flesh is given:

> We make up this whole: the flesh itself, which dies when the soul departs, is our weak part, and is not dismissed as to be fled from, but is placed aside to be received again, and when it is received, it will be abandoned no more.[125]

The soul is simply the more basic category, because it informs every deed of the flesh; so it is to the soul that responsibility for the whole is delegated.

Further, Augustine argues against a misreading of Paul's "If you live according to the flesh, you shall die." 'Flesh,' he says, is used here as a synecdoche referring to the whole man.[126] It is the confusion of these two uses of 'flesh' that leads to denigration of the flesh, and close analysis is necessary in order to ascertain whether the Apostle is using the term as synecdoche or referring specifically to the physical body. Also, Augustine admonishes his readers not only to read "In my flesh no good dwells," but also to read "No one ever hateth his own flesh, but nourishes and cherishes it, as also Christ does the Church."

> Do not be crafty in using one group of testimonies of sacred Scripture and deaf to the other, and you will be converted in both. For, if you accept these latter as they deserve, you will try to understand the former, also, in their truth.[127]

Augustine's commentators have not often been as generous to his statements as Augustine tells us here we should be with 'proof texts.' The metaphors from the early philosophical period and the polemical texts of the old Augustine are often isolated and underlined without regard for the pastoral teachings. We must, however, remember that De continentia is itself a polemical work--against the Manichaeans--so that Augustine's emphasis may be slightly distorted in that concern. Nevertheless, it is significant that Augustine would treat the very important subject of continence in the context of an anti-Manichaean polemic, and his statements about the body, although gathered to refute the Manichaeans, represent his conceptual regard for the body accurately: "How, then, is the flesh bad, when even souls themselves are advised to imitate the harmony of its members?" And: "According to each part, both soul and body, man was made good by a good God."[128]

In insisting that continence does not apply only, or even predominantly, to the body, Augustine emphasized the integral wholeness of human beings, an emphasis which we have seen was a major part of his mature theory of sensation:

> The body is by nature certainly opposed[129] to the soul, but it is not alien to the nature of man. The soul is not made up of the body, but man is made up of soul and body, and surely, whom God sets free, He sets free as a whole man. Whence the Savior Himself assumed a whole human nature, deigning to free in us the whole that He had made.[130]

In short, the soul is the true source of all incontinence and of all continence. The negativity of the virtue of continence is transcended in a positive motion of the soul: "The continence, the true continence which is from above, does not wish to repress certain evils . . . but to heal all evils through goods."[131] Instead of finding in De continentia a focus on the evil of incontinence, we find an energetic effort to point away from the body to the true seat of continence, the soul; beyond that, the goodness of the flesh is affirmed on the basis of its creation, orderliness of parts, and use in Scripture as a metaphor for the highest kind of love that the Christian faith knows, that of Christ for his Church.[132]

In De utilitate jejunii, Augustine describes the psychology of fasting: ". . . when men are hungry, they stretch out toward something; while they are stretching they are enlarged; while they are enlarged, they become capacious, and when they have become capacious enough they will be filled in due time."[133] The principle of fasting is that of "cheating the flesh" in order to effect "enrichment of the mind." De utilitate jejunii was a sermon addressed to correcting and enriching what was already a common practice of many groups in the late Roman world.

Augustine was concerned to make fasting a means to a distinctly Christian end. He is at pains, in this treatise, to combat this cultural influence. Fasting is not an end in itself as simply a repression of the body, but "we ought to direct our fasting" to the end that the spirit is strengthened by the affirmation of right order, the only way to assure, as Gilson says, that nothing will be lost. "Let the one placed over you rule you so that the one placed under you may be guided by you."[134] Fasting is a means to this end.

Also, fasting relates to being in a certain state of psychic receptivity to "heavenly food." The psychic state which accompanies fasting makes possible the kind of insight which Augustine calls "enrichment of mind." Hunger, whose psychic equivalent is longing, is 'useful' only when it can be diverted from the physical to the psychic plane.[135] In order to validate the practice in _Christian_ terms, Augustine insists that it be directed to Christian ends. _De utilitate jejunii_ from chapter vii to the end discusses the fruitlessness of fasting as an end in itself; rather, practices such as fasting achieve meaning only with spiritual ends and in the unity of the Catholic Church: ". . . let us know why we are doing what we do. By withdrawing from the joys of the flesh, the joy of the mind is gained."[136]

Again, in _De utilitate jejunii_, Augustine reminds his listeners that the body is not to be regarded as evil: "Will that flesh which is now subdued always be subdued? . . . it will not always be thus."[137] In a long and closely argued passage in chapter iv, Augustine describes the inadequacy of the view of the flesh as "at odds with the spirit." Juxtaposing Galatians 5:17, "The flesh lusteth against the spirit, and the spirit against the flesh," and Ephesians 5:29, "For no one ever hateth his own flesh, but nourishes and cherishes it, as also Christ does the Church," Augustine argues that the two apparently contradictory passages are not in opposition:

> You consider the flesh as fetters, but who loves his fetters? You consider the flesh a prison, but who loves his prison? . . . no matter how great a master of the flesh you may be, and no matter how great may be the severity toward the flesh with which you are kindled, I am inclined to think that you will close your eye if any blow threatens it.[138]

Augustine posits two reasons for fasting, and these reasons are for the purpose of appealing to two different kinds of listeners in the basilica of Hippo. Always speaking to people, for their understanding, Augustine's pastoral concern is demonstrated by his skill at recognizing and speaking to the different spiritual levels of those who listened to his sermons. For the still carnally-minded Christians, Augustine uses the incentive of fear; fasting is a method of taking one's own punishment on oneself in order to be spared by God, for it is not possible for sins to go unpunished: "I will punish myself so that He may spare me; I will take vengeance on myself so that He may come to my aid."[139] While this motivation may not seem attractive to us, and although it may seem to be prideful to "take over" one's own punishment, the principle of conscious expiation of guilt is sound psychologically. The other motive for fasting, for those who are more mature spiritually, is that of love: "Why, therefore, is it of benefit to us to abstain somewhat from food and carnal pleasure? The flesh draws one to the earth. The mind tends upward; it is caught up by love,but it is slowed down by weight."[140] The mind, when it is at the service of instinct and appetite, is not free to "live after its own nature"; one fasts to affirm the freedom of the mind to be "caught up by love." Pondeus meum, amor meus, Augustine writes in Confessions XIII.9.

Finally, the purpose of fasting is for our journey. "What this journey is and whither we are traveling must now be considered."[141] The function of fasting as a means to an end is reaffirmed, and again, as in De continentia, the negative aspect of abstinence is transcended by an essential positive motion: "I do not ask from what food you abstain, but what food you choose. Tell me what food you prefer so that I may approve your abstaining from that food."[142]

Thus, in these two treatises in which Augustine might be tempted to vent his "profound distrust of physical pleasure,"[143] Augustine's main emphasis is that of relating bodily practices to psychic states. In his 'practical' treatises, he gives evidence of a different and more comprehensive understanding of the interaction of body and soul than we find in his philosophical expositions, even in the works of his maturity. In De Trinitate XI and De genesi ad litteram XII, we find a "one-way interactionism"[144] affirmed: "Even when the soul feels pain due to some condition of the body it cannot be that the body directly causes this pain in the soul. It must be that the soul, by its own action, causes this feeling of pain within itself when there is some affliction of the body."[145] Yet in the treatises which we are discussing, the interaction described by Augustine is certainly two-way: the entire usefulness of any abstinence is benefit to the soul. Augustine would be totally without any rationale for abstinence if a two-way interactionism were not implicit. Why does Augustine fail to incorporate in his philosophical works that which he needed to assume in his practical works? We are in touch here with a real discrepancy in Augustine's thought, a failure to integrate all that he really knew.

What Augustine does consistently hold to is the pattern of right order; as the soul should be ruled by God, so the body should be ruled by the soul, but the soul's relation to the body should be "mastery, not contempt."[146] In right order there is no suggestion of repression: "The flesh, then, is not our enemy; when its vices are resisted, it itself is loved because it is cared for."[147]

We come now to the treatises which deal with the management of sexuality, _De bono coniungali_ and _De sancta virginitate_. These two treatises were written to combat the heresy of Jovinian, who denied the superiority of virginity to marriage and accused Catholics of Manichaeism because of their preference for celibacy. In answering Jovinian, Augustine had to be careful to guard his words against any trace of Manichaeism; his statements are careful but not equivocal.[148] Children are the only "worthy fruit," not of marriage, to which also the good of "natural companionship between the two sexes" attaches,[149] but of sexual intercourse. Augustine suggests that even in marriage sexual intercourse should not be considered as automatically included.[150] He says, a bit plaintively, that we do not need it for anything--except children--"For there could have been in both sexes, even without such intercourse, a kind of friendly and genuine union of the one ruling and the other obeying."[151] Married persons are "better in proportion as they begin the earlier to refrain by mutual consent from sexual intercourse."[152] It is the automatic or mechanical hegemony of sexuality that disturbs Augustine. Sexuality is a "weight" which continually threatens to overturn the precarious process of transmuting cupiditas into caritas; for a man of Augustine's temperament, moderation was more difficult than abstinence. Yet he tries hard, in De bono coniungali, to explicate the quality of a "good" which he had never experienced; discussing his thirteen-year relationship with the unnamed mother of his son, Augustine writes, "I was not so much a lover of marriage as a slave of lust."[153] I have not found a place in Augustine's writings in which he discusses marriage as anything but a "lesser good"; he arrives at this estimate by comparing it to the "good" of virginity: ". . . marriage and fornication are not two evils, the second of which is worse; but marriage and continence are two goods, the second of which is better."[154] And: "if we compare things in themselves, in no way can it be doubted that the chastity of continence is better than the chastity of marriage."[155] Although Augustine himself corrects his method of comparison with statements to the effect that "to each is given what is proper to him,"[156] and that the inner disposition of spirit is crucial whatever the state of the body,[157] his method requires its own conclusion: "in no way can it be doubted that the chastity of continence is better than the chastity of marriage." A deep ambivalence, an unresolved tension concerning sexuality is revealed in the disjunction between Augustine's method and his words:

> . . . it is not right to compare men with men in some one good. For, it can happen that one does not have something that the other has, but he has something that is to be valued more highly. [For example,] Greater, indeed, is the good of obedience than the good of continence.[158]

Augustine is very aware of the danger of comparison for the virgin. The second part of De sancta virginitate is comprised of a lengthy discussion of the uselessness of virginity which prides itself on itself: "the protector of virginity is love, but the dwelling place of this protector is humility."[159] Although the celibate "must not hesitate in the least to place this state above the other,"[160] he/she must not presume to "set herself above this or that God-fearing wife. Otherwise, she will not be humble," and "God resists the proud." In De virginitate, as in _De bono coniungali_, the contradictoriness of repeated statements concerning the worthlessness of comparisons _and_ a conclusion which rests on a comparison is never resolved. It is irreducible, and in Augustine, the skillful rhetor, points to more than an inability to organize and present an argument; it signals a pervasive ambivalence, a failure to integrate his thinking and his experience.

We need now to investigate a term that Augustine used increasingly--_concupiscentia_--for the insight it may give on Augustine's teachings on asceticism. Augustine, following St. Paul's suggestions in Galatians 5:17 that the irreducible existential dilemma of human being is the 'lust' of the flesh against the spirit, used the term _concupiscentia_ to denote this situation. Characteristically, the term is used imprecisely, and over the entire period of his writings.[161] Used interchangeably with _libido_ in Augustine's works to denote sexual desire, _concupiscentia_ has no classical usage, but is, as Bonner has shown,[162] "a Christian technical term, used exclusively by Christian writers[163] . . . with a very wide use in the Bible, generally, but not always in a bad, and sexual connotation."[164] An analysis of the passages in which Augustine uses the term would be too detailed for our purposes; the range is wide: from a good concupiscence of the soul by which it aspires to wisdom,[165] to "the passionate, uncontrolled element in sexuality."[166] Concupiscence is not a sin in itself, but a sickness,[167] a wound.[168] It comes from original sin, but is not identical with it; it is its result,[169] of which "inordinate sexual passion" is "a highly characteristic symptom," but _concupiscentia_ is not identical with sexual feeling of any kind."[170] The nature of the original fault had, for Augustine, nothing essentially to do with the creation of the body;[171] but O'Connell has discussed the ambiguity of the idea of the soul's fall in which Augustine may have been influenced by a similar ambiguity in Plotinus' concept of τόλμα: "Among other things involved in the soul's primal sin . . . is this desire to have a body, _aliquid proprium_, something _suum_--something it can independently control, and at the same time delight in controlling. Pride? or bodily 'concupiscence'?"[172]

Also, historically, the management of sexuality has always been closely associated with personal and social power; only in the last century has sexual lust and lust for power been considered separable. We must be careful of an implicit anachronism in interpreting late Roman sources in the light of twentieth century distinctions. Augustine's discussion of *libido carnalis* and *libido dominandi* in Book XIV of *De Civitate Dei* shows his linkage of the two; Bonner writes:

> Both are a consequence of the Fall, and because of our seminal identity with Adam--Omnes enim fuimus in illo uno, quando omnes fuimus ille unus (*DCD* XII.14), we are all subject to them. The Fall was a failure in obedience on the part of a created being, which was utterly dependent upon its Creator for all its powers. Disobedience, therefore, inevitably and most justly, drew upon itself a loss of control, shown both in the failure of fallen man to control his body and to resist sexual passion, and, at the same time, by a subjection to the lust to dominate others. . . . In a significant fashion, too, the twin *libidines* are brought together in the official worship of pagan Rome, with all its immodest and shameful festivals. The glories of conquest are thought to depend upon ritual obscenities, and Augustine draws particular attention to the spectacle of Cicero, *vir gravis* and *philosophaster*, who, as *aedile designate*, bore responsibility for the disgusting rites in honour of the goddess Flora.[173]

Bonner argues convincingly that Augustine's teaching on sexual concupiscence should not be studied in isolation from his doctrine of the lust for power, that these are always presented in Augustine as aspects of each other, and that they have been separated only in retrospect and as the result of a later emphasis of the Church in which "preoccupation with sexual concupiscence assumed preponderant, and at times deplorable proportions."[174] For Augustine, the management of sexuality was an aspect of a process of dealing with concupiscence, an activity of the soul, "never of the body alone, or even of the composite."[175]

Is there development in Augustine's idea of concupiscence? Thonnard, in a very careful and thorough explication of Augustine's use of *concupiscentia*, claims that Augustine's explanation in *De musica* VI.5.9 is the same as his explanation in *De civitate dei* of "the revolt of the passions, just pain of sin."[176] I think, however, that we are again in an area of Augustine's thought which shows development of emphasis rather than alteration of understanding. Also, O'Connell has demonstrated that it was "not until *De genesi contra Manichaeos* that Augustine bridged the gap between what he translates as *libido*, *concupiscentia*, and 'pride' (*superbia*)."[177] The tendency to identify concupiscence and the fall of the soul as "a kind of 'itchy desire' for sense delights and 'unclean pleasures,'" dominates Augustine's emphasis in the early works. Only in *De genesi contra Manichaeos* does he come to formulate the root fault in terms of the sins referred to in St. John's Epistle: *concupiscentia*, *curiositas*, *superbia*; his earlier attempts to explain this fault bear strong resemblances to the Manichaeans' revulsion toward sexual reproduction and their tracing of the root sin to *hûle*, as well as Plotinus' assignment of it to 'the alien principle,' matter.[178]

> It is not, therefore, surprising that Augustine's first serious efforts to seek out a definition of sin start with the terms *libido* and *cupiditas* (*Lib*. I.8. flg.), and . . . his later efforts . . . make this emphasis rhyme with the more Christian *superbia*.[179]

But with his conceptual resolution of the root-fault along Scriptural lines, another development occurs which is crucial to our understanding of Augustine's use of *concupiscentia* and his teaching on asceticism. No longer is concupiscence something to be overcome once and for all, in order that the Christian can possess the *beata vita*.[180] With his increasing understanding of Scripture, Augustine came to change his emphasis from the body as tainted with metaphysical evil to the body as experiential limitation on immediate and permanent happiness. Not until the *body* can fully share in redemption can the Christian truly experience beatitude. The ambivalence is heightened and intensified: on the one hand the life of the body is valued more highly; it is no longer enough to enjoy delights of the mind; yet the body then becomes absolute limitation.[181]

In addition, Athanase Sage points out what he calls a "Copernican transposition . . . one of the most original traits of the thought of St. Augustine:[182] With the *De Genesi ad litteram*, the order of precedence between mortality and concupiscence is reversed." From 412 on, "the *reatus* which accompanies concupiscence is identified with original sin."[183] The 'sickness,' no longer adventitious, is not individually acquired, but precedes and undermines each human being's life. Thus, infants like adults require baptism in remissionem peccatorum. The weight of concupiscence becomes immeasurably greater, its effect more pervasive, so that only a part of it is removed by baptism; the penalty remains: "in a more and more explicit way, Augustine insisted that concupiscence remains, although original sin is totally removed by baptism."[184]

But the accusation of Manichaeism by writers, some even in Augustine's own time, came from a confusion between his descriptions of the almost continuous struggle within human beings, and his descriptions of what constitutes the metaphysical essence of human being. Like Paul, whose antithesis of flesh and spirit "is a moral and not a metaphysical distinction," Augustine posits a "moral conflict within the human soul, not an encounter of opposing substances."[185] It is because of this moral conflict, this permanent struggle between 'flesh' and 'spirit' that Augustine teaches asceticism. Asceticism is a method for the gathering and focusing of psychic energy; yet it is emphatically not a matter of 'will power' but requires, and is a gift of, Divine help.[186]

iii

It is with the question of concupiscence that we can make a transition to discussing Augustine's later teaching on asceticism, since the notion was so constantly discussed in the Pelagian controversy. Although it was not the main issue in this controversy, it was the dramatic one.[187] There is no doubt that the old Augustine narrowed his working definition of concupiscentia to sexuality. Until Julian's entrance in the Pelagian controversy, the question of sexuality had been decidedly secondary to that of original sin and infant baptism in remissionem peccatorum. We must be careful to place influence and result in the proper order: the actual practice of the Church in baptising infants was "prior to" and "largely stimulated" the growth of the doctrine of original sin.[188] Augustine's defense and elaboration of the doctrine of original sin in the context of the Pelagian controversy must be read as the defense and elaboration by a churchman of a pivotal sacramental practice.[189] It is essential to understand the extent to which, after 415, Augustine had become a churchman: ". . . after a decade of profound, inconclusive and highly personal speculations, Augustine will suddenly pour his ideas into a solid mould. He will identify them entirely with the unquestioned faith of the Catholic church."[190] Augustine was aware of his authority and could assume others were.[191] The question, for Augustine, was not whether the church _should_ be powerful; rather, the question was how to manage the rapidly increasing power and authority of the church. From 415 on, Augustine will restrain speculative tendencies in favor of pastoral and polemical concerns. The controversy with Pelagius marks the turning point. Convinced by the success of the conflict with Donatism, Augustine openly used all the implements of an unabashed power struggle to effect a suppression of Pelagius and Caelestius.[192] He focused on bolstering Catholic practice with supporting theory.

It is in this context that we can begin to understand the controversy with Julian. We need to place sexuality in the context in which Augustine himself placed it in this debate, that is, as an _indication_, along with the massive sufferings of the human race, of concupiscence, the primal and undifferentiated lust for pleasure without orientation to God. But a more subtle point arises: Samuel Laeuchli, in _Power and Sexuality_, has pointed out the symbiotic relationship between management of sexuality and structures of social power. The old Augustine's preoccupation with personal and ecclesiastical power is at the same time a commensurate preoccupation with the management of sexuality. It is not only Julian's pressure on the subject which determined its importance to the controversy. Seen in its broadest social consequences, the Pelagian controversy was over the kind of church that would develop--a communion of intellectual and ascetic _perfecti_, or a church of 'middle-brow'[193] Christians. Also, a church which is reworking its image from the unambiguous definition of a persecuted body to a major social and political grouping needs new methods of differentiation from the culture. Strong norms for sexual behavior provide exactly this sort of definition of who is a Christian and who is not.[194] The legislation of morality is one of the first impulses of a power-oriented organization: "the empire itself had taken violent measures to fight the widespread practices of divorce and adultery (Cod. Just. IX.9.2). The categorizing of extremely limited sexuality as part of an ideal about man certainly was as present in the rival movements as in the Christian church."[195] In addition, the celibacy of the clergy[196] was crucially important to the "clerical leadership image."[197] Tertullian had argued that sexual purity and priestly power belong together.[198] The celibacy of the priesthood was also an important emancipation from the culture; "By being born, by being suckled, and then by marrying one was constantly being reminded of being drawn back into what was stable, rooted, and enveloping."[199] Even stronger ties to the culture and business of the community are inevitable in having children. Augustine insisted on the celibacy and seclusion of his clergy from the community.[200]

One of the most telling aspects of the later Pelagian controversy was the way in which it engaged popular interest; it is impossible to assess exactly how widespread this interest was, but we can certainly discern the beginnings of the man-on-the-street involvement which would soon characterize the great controversies of the mid-fifth century. There is evidence that Augustine purposely popularized the conflict;[201] he appealed specifically to an audience of 'average Catholics,' and billed Julian as an 'intellectual,' "bent on troubling the faith of simple military men . . . . [and] a man who thought himself above the healthy feelings of the man in the street."[202] The popularization of the debate is important because it determined not only the intellectual level on which it could be conducted, but even more importantly, the issues that will be raised. A popular debate cannot, in any age, rise much above the level of "Is it good or bad?" and, indeed, we have found Augustine saying precisely that: "the whole point between us in this controversy is whether the thing (sexuality) of which good use is made is good or evil."[203] We have only to analyze a popular controversy of our own time--recognition of homosexuals--to see that the "whole point" of the statements on both sides is whether homosexuality is good or bad! A great deal of what disturbs us about this 'unintelligent slogging-match'[204] can be directly attributed to Augustine's deliberate attempt to popularize it. He tremendously flattered the 'average Catholic' by rendering the debate accessible to him and calling upon him to judge it; Julian will rage in vain that "the helm of reason has been wrenched from the Church, so that the opinions of the mob can sail ahead with all flags flying."[205]

Finally, it is apparent from Augustine's treatment of *libido dominandi* and *libido carnalis* in Book XIV.15, 16, and 17 of *De civitate Dei*, that he did not assume or envision any division between them. Bonner attributes the eventual conceptual separation of the lust for power and sexual lust as explicable in part by the "historical circumstances" of his writings. While writing to Christians, he tends, especially in the Pelagian controversy, to stress the aspect of *concupiscentia carnalis*; his apologetic works, primarily directed to a pagan audience, stressed *libido dominandi*:

> As a consequence, once the triumph of Christianity was assured, moral theologians turned to the anti-pelagian writings for doctrine regarding the *libido carnalis*, while the *libido dominandi*, of interest largely to the stateman and political theorist, was very much left out of account where the individual was concerned.[206]

But let us look at several writings of the later Pelagian controversy period, *De civitate Dei* XIV (A.D. 418-420), *De nuptiis et concupiscentia* (420-421), *Contra Julianum* (421-422), and *Opus imperfectum contra Julianum* (to 430), with a specific question in mind: what development of emphasis can be discerned in these writings?

The purpose of *De nuptiis et concupiscentia*, Augustine tells us in the preface to *Contra Julianum*, was to "distinguish the good of marriage from the evil of concupiscence."[207] Through the painstaking circumlocutions and distinctions of this treatise, the premise and the conclusion are the irreducible evil inherent in sexuality as we know it. But again and again he stresses that we know it only in its fallen condition, that before the sin of Adam and Eve, sexuality could have been totally without lust and in the service of reason;[208] he describes a situation in which body and soul would be kept "together," not an etiolated pleasureless sexuality.[209] His problem is how to use well the 'evil' that is our fallen sexuality, disjunctive and incongruent with reason. There is, however, a discernible hardening of his view of sexuality:

> . . . twenty years previously, in the mellow mood that had coincided with the writing of the Confessions, Augustine had even gone so far as to suggest, with great sensitivity, that the quality of sexual intercourse itself might be modified and transformed by the permanent friendship of two people in marriage. Now, however, he will isolate sexual intercourse as an element of evil encapsulated in every marriage.[210]

The real problem with concupiscence is not any particular state of excitation of the body, but the existential reality that concupiscence falls outside the purview of the will and therefore notoriously resists integration. Augustine's description of our disjunctive sexuality in De civitate Dei XIV.16 makes this clear; the fact of impotence is as distressing and significant an aspect of concupiscence as excitation:

> Sometimes the impulse is an unwanted intruder, sometimes it abandons the eager lover, and desire cools off in the body while it is still at boiling heat in the mind. Thus strangely does lust refuse to be a servant not only to the will to beget but even to the lust for lascivious indulgence; and although on the whole it is totally opposed to the mind's control, it is quite often divided against itself. It arouses the mind, but does not follow its own lead by arousing the body.[211]

Augustine's imaginative eulogy of sexual activity before the Fall, in XIV.26, also stresses that "the sexual organs would have been brought into activity by the same bidding of the will as controlled the other organs."[212]

But in De civitate Dei XIV, written between 418 and 420, Augustine has not yet arrived at the emphasis he will come to in the heat of the controversy with Julian. His conclusion:

> I do not say that children, coming from an evil action are evil, since I do not say that the activity in which married persons engage for the purpose of begetting children is evil. As a matter of fact, I assert that it is good, because it makes good use of the evil of lust, and through this good use, human beings, a good work of God, are generated. But the action is not performed without evil . . . .[213]

A truly ambiguous statement! But Augustine is very clear as to where blame belongs: "I say to you in the highest truth that the evil with which a person is born is not the fruit of bodies, sexes, and union for these are goods whose author is God; it is the fruit of the first prevarication."[214] Concupiscence is punished by "wholly natural connections" for the sin of Adam in which the whole human race participated, not vicariously, but by 'actual identity' with him: "For we were all in that one person, seeing that we all _were_ that one person."[215]

N. P. Williams has emphasized some positive ramifications of the doctrine of the Fall and original sin which we should note here because these considerations are operative in Augustine's thought and affect his teaching on asceticism. First, it is significant that fall theory shows its strongest development and elaboration in precisely the historic periods in which the church has felt the need to combat a wave of pessimism or dualism:

> It is the idea of the Fall, with its necessary implication of the contingency and temporality, as opposed to the eternity and necessity, of evil, which makes all the difference: without the belief in the Fall, the doctrine of Original Sin _is_ Manichaeism . . . the Fall theory and dualism _are_ in principle, and always have been in history, mutually exclusive hypotheses.[216]

Second, Williams has shown that:

> the doctrine of 'inherited infirmity' would seem to be a merciful rather than a rigorist conception; as compared with the unlimited indeterminism of Pelagius it makes a deliberate allowance for human frailty and to a certain extent diminishes, though it does not abolish, man's responsibility for actual sin.[217]

For Augustine, as for St. Paul, the evil in human life is a necessary conclusion from the evidence of gratuitous suffering[218] and the frustration of a fallen sexuality which eludes complete integration. Pelagianism, in fact, "does not minimize the sense of sin but exacerbates it."[219] If perfection is possible, perfection is mandatory. It is curious to notice the juxtaposition in Pelagianism of the affirmation of the good of sexuality as we experience it and the underlying absolute moral demand for 'perfection,' for the perfect integration of sexuality and rationality. Augustine finds this ideal visionary. Christian asceticism is a gift of God; yet asceticism, and especially celibacy, does not, in the old Augustine, have the assumption of moral neutrality that a 'gift'--given or withheld--might imply; rather: "The evil of carnal concupiscence is so great that it is better to refrain from using it than to use it well."[220]

The emphasis, significantly full of quotations from Ambrose, is on the flesh as a "dangerous adversary"; the Christian life is imaged as war: "whoever does not wish to serve lust must war against it; whoever neglects the fight must serve it."[221] But Augustine's metaphors reveal a contradiction: often they are medical, in a very modern sense: concupiscentia is sickness, not sin; his model of health is frankly imaginative: "When occasion for lusting arises, yet no evil desire is excited, not even against our will, we have full health."[222]

> When I say this concupiscence is a disease, why do you deny it, if you concede that a remedy for it is necessary? If you acknowledge the remedy, acknowledge the disease. If you deny the disease, deny the remedy. . . . No one provides a remedy for health.[223]

But we do not find the old Augustine urging ever more stringent ascetic practices. Asceticism does not begin to get at the root of the problem. At best, when motivated by caritas, it purifies and clarifies the soul. It is significant that Augustine's late teaching on sexuality, the Fall, and original sin, does not result in an intensification of ascetic teaching. Concupiscentia is existential. It is the operational condition and emotional evidence of a radical disjunction in human nature, a contradiction, insulting to human reason, between our actions, which are rationally chosen and painstakingly designed to ensure our happiness, and the fact that this happiness does not follow from our actions.

In conclusion, we can summarize Augustine's view on asceticism: in the early period, he was attracted to the standard philosophical injunctions to ascetic living; the emphasis is entirely on what sort of life-style best promotes the life of the mind. In his mature writings on asceticism, Augustine emphasizes only celibacy among the practices he discusses, but reveals the tension of ambivalence between his conceptual treatment of the body and sexuality as the good creation of the good God, and its decidedly problematic affiliation with concupiscentia. The later writings, while apparently focusing on sexuality, actually use the issue as the testing ground for other issues: the power and the authority of the Church and the question of whether the

Church will be the bastion of intellectual specialists or a layman's church. In all, we can agree with A. Hilary Armstrong's summary of Augustine's teaching on asceticism: "Augustine, whatever the defects of his thought in this or other ways at any period of his life, when seen in the context of his own time and compared with his contemporaries, appears on the whole like other Christian Platonists, moderate, humane, and positive in his attitude to this world and to the body."[224]

CHAPTER IV

THE DEVELOPMENT OF AUGUSTINE'S VIEW OF THE INCARNATION AND THE EFFECT OF THIS VIEW ON HIS EVALUATION OF THE MEANING AND VALUE OF THE BODY

Augustine's attempt to understand and describe the dogma of the Incarnation was an aspect of his conscious effort to achieve an adequate description of the way in which body and soul can participate in human incarnate being. The conceptual problem was imposed on Augustine both as a secular man of his time in a universe of discourse in which the question of the unity of body and soul was a focus of discussion, and as a churchman who had trouble explaining the Incarnation, not only to pagans, but even to his congregation.

The problem of the relationship of body and soul had been analyzed and discussed since Aristotle; the Christian dogma of the Incarnation fell heir to both the tools and the difficulties with which philosophers had been dealing for centuries in the attempt to explain the relationship of body and soul. C. N. Cochrane describes the ramifications of this problem and concludes that it was never satisfactorily resolved in ancient classicism. The major attempts to describe the relationship were made by Aristotle, the Stoics, and the Platonists:

> . . . on the one hand it is possible to regard this body as ultimate, i.e., the real principle of our existence as human beings. This, indeed, is the way in which the body presents itself to the naive intelligence. . . . On the other hand body might be resolved, as it was by the Platonists, into mere 'appearance,' deriving such reality as it possessed from a world of self-subsistent forms beyond itself.[1]

Neither of the classical answers adequately accounts for the experiential integrated activity of body and soul. In the Stoic account which limits real existence to bodies, consciousness becomes "a kind of epiphenomenon."[2] The Platonic account is open to Aristotle's criticism of Plato's doctrine of the Ideas: "Unless the ideal world and the sensible world can be united . . . the Ideas are a useless duplication of objects."[3]

> To Augustine, these alternatives are equally unsatisfactory; body is neither absolute reality nor absolute appearance; it is the organ by which mankind establishes contact with the objective world.[4]

But let us examine more carefully these descriptions; they form the background and, in some aspects, were directly borrowed by patristic authors from classicism to describe the Incarnation. We will first look briefly at the Stoic account of the relation of body and soul, then at the Platonic, and, finally, at the patristic authors before moving to Augustine's own development in understanding the Incarnation.

Aristotle, the "first to raise the question as to what constitutes the unity of body and soul,"[5] had complained that although all the Platonists believe that body and soul are one (ἕν), they did not explain "in virtue of what . . . the soul and the body are one."[6] Aristotle's own resolution of the problem was that "if, as we say, one element is matter and another is form, and one is potentially, and the other actually, the question will no longer be thought a difficulty," because "it is the nature of matter and form to unite with each other and become one."[7] "Soul and body are therefore one because soul is the form of the body."[8] Aristotle thought it imperative to examine the nature of the soul/body relation, and thinkers after him accepted this task as primary to their philosophies. The importance of analyzing it lay in the fact that: "it is by this association that the one acts and the other is acted upon, that the one moves and the other is moved; and no such mutual relation is found in haphazard combinations."[9] Aristotle then proceeded to enumerate the various ways in which things can combine to form a unity.

Apparently using Aristotle's work as a basis, the Stoics developed a threefold classification of ways in which things may form unities: juxtaposition (παράφεσις), as illustrated by "heaps of wheat, barley, lentils . . . [or] the pebbles and sand of the seashore";[10] mixture (κρᾶσις), a "mutual" coextension of dissimilar parts entering into one another at all points," like wine and water, in which the two elements are at least theoretically resolvable into the constituent parts; and the third kind of union, called "confusion" (σύγχυσις), "the corruption of all original distinctive qualities, owing to their component parts penetrating one another at every point, so as to generate one thing wholly different."[11] These modes of combination all refer to the union of physical things since, for the Stoics, the criterion of the real existence of things was that they "must be capable of producing or experiencing some change," a condition met only by bodies. But bodies, by definition, are already a compound of the active principle, λόγος, and the passive principle, matter; "in Stoicism, matter and the active shaping principle never exist apart from one another. Together they constitute all that exists, and they can only be drawn apart for the purpose of conceptual analysis."[12] The mode in which logos and matter are combined in bodies is 'mixture': "God is mixed with matter, penetrates the whole of matter, and shapes it."[13] For both Aristotle and the Stoics there is an interrelationship, if not an interdependence, between the active and the passive principles. Yet they are not reducible to one principle;[14] nor are they antagonistic: ". . . at that time our body/spirit antinomie did not exist."[15] Yet while the Stoic formulation overtly favored monism, the dualism is implicit, strongly felt, and emerged more and more in the ethics of later Stoicism. Long before Augustine's time a marked uneasiness with 'mixture' emerged in Stoicism.[16] The longing to differentiate the components of human being pervades late Roman philosophy and religion.

The Manichaeans gave a fully articulated conceptual formulation to this antipathy to undifferentiated 'mixture.' The tremendous relief which must have come through giving such a conceptual framework to experience is described by Simone Pétrement as the 'violent and joyful' aspect of Gnosticism;[17] sin is clearly defined and the origins of its crippling effects designated: "sin originates in the soul's immersion in mixture . . . the soul does not succumb to sin through its own impulsion, but through its mixture with the flesh."[18] In addition, suffering and struggle--the greatest conceptual difficulties for a monistic system--receive a facile explanation: there is "an unalterable material foundation for the inequity of human souls with regard to the possibility of redemption: the degree of the soul's consciousness is the foundation of the degree of mixture."[19] The visible world thus "becomes a 'giant pharmacy' for the distillation of light from the 'shameful mixture.'"[20] The docetist view of the Incarnation held by the Manichaeans follows logically from their cosmology. This view "was not so much the negation of the divinity of Christ as the separation of the two natures--the divinity and the human nature--in Christ."[21]

For Plotinus also, the origin of 'ugliness' is "the admixture of disorderly passions derived from too close association with the body, and it is the soul itself in its unmixed nature that is beautiful."[22] His concern with psychology thus requires the effort "to discover which psychological functions belong to the soul in her pure state and which arise as a consequence of her embodiment."[23] As discussed above, Plotinus' discussions of the relationship of soul and body occur in the contexts of "attempts to preserve the soul from substantial disturbance."[24] While the soul gives the body a share in her own life, this activity is not a real participation by the soul in the body's life: "change and disturbance have their seat in the animated body and do not touch the soul herself."[25] For reasons of wishing to link the emotions and the physical constitution, Plotinus took interest in Galen's medical work and Aristotle's references to "the influence of man's bodily constitution and of the climatic and other forces . . . on the irrational soul."[26] Plotinus had inherited the discussion of this relationship from the Middle Platonists' attempt to answer the Stoic rejection of the possibility of any relation between a corporeal and a spiritual entity: "Plotinus takes great pains . . . to refute the Stoic view that the soul is a special kind of body, the πνεῦμα in a particular state."[27] In addition, Plotinus rejected the conclusion of Aristotle that the soul is the 'form' of the body.[28] In his major discussion of the relation of body and soul, Ennead IV.3.20, he makes use of the theory, apparently originated by Ammonius Saccas, of unio inconfusa (ἄμικτος, ἀσύγχυτος ἕνωσις), to describe this relation. While there is something alien about the body to the soul since it, as a spiritual substance, is fully capable of existing without the body, body, on the other hand, "has what Plotinus calls an 'aptitude' (ἐπιτηδειότης)[29] for soul."[30] In spite of the aspect of burdensomeness of the body, there is, in the Plotinian system, a 'universal law,'

> that the higher must give itself to the lower, and that soul must impart itself to body in order to realize its own implicit powers and to contribute to the perfection of the Cosmos. This means that the 'sin' of the soul in entering the body proves to be, as it were, the '*felix culpa*' that is necessary to the divine economy. The incarnation of the soul is therefore no more the result of genuine sin than is the casting of a shadow.[31]

This positive view of incarnation was important to Christian philosophers such as Augustine in formulating a suitable description of the incarnate human condition and in their struggle to describe the Incarnation of the 'Word made flesh.' Although Plotinus insisted on a nonspatial understanding of the unity of body and soul, he offers one metaphor of this unity--a spatial one: the true relation of soul and body, he says, is analogous to that of light and air:

> Light is both present and not present to air, for though it completely penetrates the air, it is not blended with it at any point. While the air flows past, it remains immobile; and when air passes beyond the region of illumination, it takes no light away from it. Therefore, just as the air is in the light and not vice-versa, the body is in the soul and not the soul in the body. But there is no objection to saying that the soul is 'present to' the body, as long as we do not imply that any mixture has taken place between them. The soul is no more mixed with the body than light with air.[32]

Yet an analogy is not a scientific explanation. In *Ennead* I.1, the last of Plotinus' psychological writings, he is still struggling to arrive at an explanation. His theory of sensation is the connecting link between body and soul in that sensation does not occur without the participation of both: "Body by itself is inert and soul by itself is impassible."[33] The "connecting link" is thus an activity, an activity of the soul which uses the body as a craftsman uses a tool. There is no confusion or mixture of substances,[34] but there is participation of the unmodified components in an activity.[35]

Trying, then, to define an overall tone in Plotinus' description of the relation of soul and body, we find the strongest statements oriented to description of this relation which is nonpejorative to the body; but context is all: in II.9, his defense of the physical world against the Gnostics is unequivocal, but in his remarks on the subject of reincarnation, he tends to emphasize the ill effects of the body on the soul. The net effect of Plotinus' statements is to continue and deepen the Platonic ambivalence toward incarnation.

The patristic authors, faced with the task of describing the Incarnation of the Word, inherited both the difficulties of the philosophers' problem of describing the relationship of body and soul, and many of their conceptual tools. The differing understandings of Christ's corporeality of the Eastern and Western fathers became apparent quite early. Although Clement of Alexandria wrote: "no true digestion and elimination of food took place in the Lord,"[36] an idea he apparently took over from Valentinus,[37] Tertullian, the first of the fathers to discuss the Incarnation along philosophic lines, emphasized Christ's physicality almost to the point of crudity. "It was," he writes in *De carne Christi*, "precisely the non-marvelous character of His terrestrial flesh which made the rest of His activities things to marvel at."[38] It is in Tertullian that we find the emphasis on the Incarnation of Christ as the direct source of the redemption of the whole human being: "If Christ came forth for the purpose of delivering not our flesh but our soul alone, in the first place how absurd it is that when intending to deliver the soul alone, He should have made it into that sort of body which he was not going to deliver."[39] Tertullian addressed the question of whether the Incarnation can be described properly as a *tertium quid*, the result of the confusion of flesh and spirit in Jesus; if this were the case, "there would be no distinct proofs apparent of either nature."[40] Rather, "we see plainly the twofold state not confounded but conjoined (*conjunctum*) in one person (*una persona*)--Jesus, God and man." Tertullian also, in other passages, used the term 'mixture' to describe the relation: "man mixed (*mixtus*) with God,"[41] or as "mixing (*miscente*) in Himself man and God."[42] For Tertullian there is no real difficulty with the Incarnation[43] because the assumption of the corporeality of the soul meant it could freely join with body.[44]

The eastern patristic authors, on the other hand, emphasized the subsumption of the human by the divine in Christ. Origen states, in Contra Celsum, in response to Celsus' charge that Christians regard Jesus "who was but a mortal body" as God:

> He whom we regard and believe to have been from the beginning God and the son of God is the true Logos and the true Wisdom and the very Truth; and with respect to His mortal body and the human soul which it contained, we assert that not by their communion merely with Him, but by their union (ἑνώσει) and intermingling (ἀνακράει) they receive the highest powers, and after participating in His divinity, were changed into God.[45]

This "union of predominance" in which the Logos, the stronger component, completely subsumes the weaker, the 'mortal body,' without itself undergoing alteration, is explained by Origen "by the analogy of Aristotle's theory of the unity of matter and form, thus reflecting Aristotle's own comparison of the relation of the weaker to the stronger element in a 'union of predominance' to the relation of matter and form."[46] It is Wolfson's judgment that when the "orthodox fathers use the term 'mixture' without any clarifying comment, it is also in the sense of 'predominance' that it is used by them."[47]

Yet it is important to note that the pervasive philosophy underlying the early fathers' description of the Incarnation was Stoicism, that "at that time . . . . Platonism had not yet made a come-back."[48] And Stoicism, not positing a disjunction between body and soul, conceptualized such a 'union of predominance' differently than a Platonist would, that is, not as a spiritualization of the body, but as a perfect integration of components under the hegemony of the spirit, the living, active, creative element. One must not oversimplify Origen's tendency to present the corporeality of Christ as a "filter" of the Logos, "a concealment of the Godhead";[49] he shows "in his interpretation of the Transfiguration scene how the Godhead becomes transparent precisely in the corporeality of Jesus." He also duplicates Tertullian's argument, quoted above: "The whole man would not have been redeemed had He not assumed the whole man."[50]

In the fourth century, the characteristic form of the question concerning the Incarnation was: "were the human sufferings of Christ real or not?"[51] The nature of the Incarnation became an intensified question.[52] In Latin christology, the two natures theme dominates; in Greek, the idea of unity.[53] For Arius as for Ambrose, the question was one of composition, "how God could enter into combination with nature."[54] Here the anthropological analogy was applied: "for the theologians of the time it was the supreme example of the unity of two substances."[55] For Athanasius, midway between the Arians and the Apollinarians, the relation of Logos and world, soul and body, is analogous to that of Logos and body in Christ. Thus, the λόγος-σάρξ emphasis which omits from the Incarnation a human soul dictates Athanasius' "remarkable procedure of making the 'flesh' of Christ the physical subject of experiences that normally have their place in the soul."[56] The body of Christ is the instrument of the Logos (ὄργανον), a slight variation of the union of predominance theme.

The Cappadocians continue to deal with the Incarnation in response not to the great christological controversies of Arianism and Apollinarianism, but in response to local errors of interpretation. While concerned to maintain the unity and distinctness of the two natures in Christ, they never arrived at a description which did full justice to Christ's humanity.[57] They used the Stoic description of 'mixture' to describe the unity of Christ, and it is clear that it is in the sense of a union of predominance. Gregory of Nazianzus writes:

> The man below became God after he had become commixed (συνανεκρά) with God and, by the victory of that which is more potent (τοῦ κρείπονος), he became one.[58]

> The slowness with which the Greek fathers of the fourth century struggled through to a full recognition of the humanity of the Lord may well be a result of the struggle against Arianism. . . . But the decisive factor was something quite different. Some fathers had an unsatisfactory picture of Christ in which the manhood of Jesus was not given its due place.[59]

Ambrose, Augustine's most direct mentor in the early years of his conversion, used a combination of Stoic, Neoplatonic, and Greek patristic authors to deal with the mystery of the

Incarnation. That it was problematic for him is a necessary assumption from his anthropology in which "it is not possible to be at home with God and with the flesh at the same time."[60] He holds this view of the body in tension with a positive view of the Incarnation of the Word:

> For what was the cause of the Incarnation except that flesh which had sinned might be redeemed through itself?[61]
>
> Why did Christ descend except that that flesh of yours might be cleansed, the flesh which He took over from our condition?[62]

It is in Ambrose that we find the distinction between metaphysical description and existential reality most clearly drawn; the body, while a "superb work of divine art," is nonetheless "the enemy of the soul." Metaphysically, the body is real and good in its own right; experientially, "what is according to the nature of the body is contrary to the nature of the soul."[63] The Incarnation is no longer a union of predominance in which Logos subsumes humanity, but Ambrose clearly distinguishes between the divine and the human work of Christ (*operis distinctione*), while insisting on unity of person (*non varietate personae*).[64] He handles the problem of describing the distinction of two natures in Christ by distinguishing "the levels on which unity and distinction in Christ are to be sought,"[65] not as an explanation of the Incarnation so much as a way to bypass the problem. The *unio inconfusa* of the Neoplatonists served Ambrose in distinguishing the two natures in Christ: "the Lord, coming in our flesh, joined together the Godhead and flesh without any confusion or mixture." Dudden concludes his discussion of Ambrose's christology with the remark that "Ambrose can't explain how two complete natures can be united in one person, but he affirms it."[66]

The λόγος-ἄνθρωπος emphasis, which would later develop into the full Antiochean position, championed in the West by Hilary, acknowledged the full manhood of Christ and his true Godhead. Yet echoes of the 'union of predominance' persist; Hilary sees, in all the earthly activity of Christ, a "mixing of divine and human . . . until finally the Godhead is fully revealed and the humanity of Christ is virtually overwhelmed by the Godhead."[67] Jerome's *Tractatus sive homiliae in*

Psalmus 108 goes further than Hilary in "daring to speak of passiones and libidines in Christ."[68]

We come now to examine Augustine's developing view of the Incarnation. In doing this, we will explore O'Connell's suggestion that his understanding emerges through three basic stages[69]--an early unexamined Antiochean view, the Confessions' Alexandrine critique of the earlier position, and a mature understanding of una persona which was the result of laborious personal efforts.[70] We will find that while this description of Augustine's developing christology is accurate, it does not do justice to the richness of the picture.

The texts of A.D. 386-391 which deal with the Incarnation present it as nonproblematic, a union of predominance along the lines of the earlier fathers. One senses that he has not yet realized the difficulty involved in genuinely integrating the dogma of the Incarnation and so can present it in unexplored formulae:[71]

> 'I came from the Father and I came into the world' . . . appearing to men in a man, when the Word was made flesh and lived among us. This does not mean that there has been a change of God's nature, but it means the taking of the nature of inferior persons, that is, human beings.[72]

Augustine himself, reviewing this early period in the Confessions, admitted his lack of understanding[73] and his eagerness to identify Plotinus' 'Intellect' with the Christian 'Word'; since it was exactly the Incarnation of the Word that he did not find in Neoplatonism, he had no prepared philosophical interpretation to bring to it.[74] Both the texts of the early period and Augustine's analysis of his understanding in Confessions VII.19.25 support his statement that his early picture was of the λόγος-ἄνθρωπος type, and tended to the Photinian variation of this emphasis in which the insistence on Christ's humanity was so strong that Augustine says he saw Christ as a man "to be preferred above all other men, because of some great excellence of his human nature and a more perfect participation in wisdom."[75]

Although Augustine clearly affirms the Incarnation in the works prior to A.D. 391, his focus in these works is philosophical rather than theological; none of the texts listed in the

Dictionnaire de Théologie Catholique as important statements of Augustine on the Incarnation occurs in this period. The pattern the statements on the Incarnation follow is that which we saw Ambrose following: affirmation without understanding. "The Incarnation is, for the new convert, a sublime, ineffable mystery, inaccessible to the proud, and a proof of divine mercy."[76]

The two dominant themes of Augustine's early view of the Incarnation are (1) the distinctness of the two natures in Christ, and (2) the image of the humanity of Christ as a mask for his divinity. The two are not integrated in this period. We recognize in the first the influence of Latin christology and Ambrose's direct influence, discussed above. Augustine's later description in Confessions VII.19.25 elucidated his feeling of the necessity for this distinction: it was clear to him that the activities of Christ on earth--eating, speaking, sleeping, etc.--were all "marks of a soul and a mind which are mutable,"[77] and so could not possibly be the functions of the immutable Word. Augustine writes, "I did now know this without having any doubt about it all."[78] Yet the Cassiciacum Augustine, no doubt with the recent struggle of Ambrose against the Arians in mind, also affirms the divinity of Christ; Christ is "truly God,"[79] the divine Intellect itself.[80] Augustine was equipped with philosophical tools to understand the distinction of the two natures in Christ; how does he image Christ's unity? Hominem suscipere,[81] susceptio inferioris personae,[82] naturam humanam suscipere--these are some of the expressions used in the early period to express the mystery of the Incarnation. We will see that Augustine actively deepens and renders precise his understanding of persona, but in the early period it conceals his acknowledged inability to penetrate the mystery of the Incarnation.[83]

At Cassiciacum, the union of divinity and humanity is explicitly mentioned only three times and, as O'Connell has found, "In all three instances . . . the stress is placed on the enormous divine condescension involved, on the difficulty some might have in believing that divinity could so closely associate with bodily humanity."[84] The Incarnational texts up to the time of the Confessions demonstrate Augustine's struggle to arrive at an understanding and formulation for Christ's unity.

His frustration may be indicated by the use of a curious term, _homo dominicus_, which he discontinued after A.D. 395 and criticized in the _Retractationes_ as not expressing adequately the unity of Christ.[85] It is significant that the search for a formula occurs frequently in the context of discussing the uniqueness of Christ over the saints who were also filled with the wisdom of God.[86] It is in this context that the term _persona_ serves to designate Christ's uniqueness: "It is one thing," he writes in _De Agone Christiano_, "to become wise through the Divine wisdom, and another thing to bear the very _persona_ of the Divine wisdom."[87] Yet as early as A.D. 391, in what is thought to be Augustine's first sermon after his ordination to the priesthood, he presents what Grillmeier calls "a comparatively comprehensive formula whose affinity to the most moderate Antiochene theology is striking":

> For as a matter of fact, complete manhood, that is, rational soul and body, was assumed by the Word so that the Word, the son of God might be not only Christ, not only God, but also man, being in his entirety the Son of God the Father because he is the Word, and the Son of Man because of his humanity. . . . At the same time that he is man, he is the Son of God because he is the Word by whom human nature was assumed; at the same time that he is the Word, he is the Son of Man because of the human nature assumed by the Word.[88]

The picture is not one of slow but constant progression toward an adequate Incarnational formula. O'Connell has argued that the works following the Cassiciacum dialogues make use of the Antiochean formula which Augustine indicts in the _Confessions_ far more than do the Cassiciacum works: "Instead of moving _away_, as one might have hoped, the writings stretching from A.D. 387-391 show Augustine steadily advancing toward an even firmer expression of the Incarnation theory he was later brought to condemn."[89] Had it been simply a matter of coming to understand and affirm a traditional formula of the Catholic Church, Augustine would have adhered to this formula and labored to assimilate it. He did operate thus on the Trinitarian formula, rejecting "Plotinian subordinationism." But Incarnational theology had not achieved a comprehensive understanding of the person of Christ, so Augustine tended far more to bring to it disparate tools for understanding.

> But what did the Church hold on the mystery of the Incarnation? Here confusion of minds was possible--and widespread. Alypius' attribution of Apollinarianism to the Catholic Church is only one instance of that regnant state of things.[90]

Thus Augustine worries over the Incarnation, not comfortable with his formulation until about A.D. 412, the first clear statement of the theory which he held subsequently; although even in De quantitate animae the expression neque discrete, neque confusa occurs, Augustine does not apply it to the Incarnation; but even as late as De vera religione,[91] images the Incarnation in Plotinian terms of descent and return. The "sharp distinction" between the man, Jesus Christ and the Wisdom that fills him remains.

> But the expression used to couch the distinction is not at all reassuring: praise must be given to the Divine Wisdom, but the man Jesus, for his part, would surely merit something of 'his own' (proprium). He would occupy an eminence 'above all other men.' These phrases are far closer to the Confessions' indictment than any to be found in the Cassiciacum writings.[92]

This is partly accounted for by the fact that Augustine has different concerns in the dialogues than in the subsequent theological works. The dialogues are just that--dialogues in the philosophic tradition and on topics of philosophical concern. O'Connell has omitted part of the richness of the picture in his concern to document Augustine's Neoplatonism.[93] The broader interpretation of Augustine's apparent lack of insight and instability in his Incarnational teaching before A.D. 412 has partly to do with the differing audiences to which he addressed himself, and partly to the chaotic state of Incarnational theology in his time. The Augustine of the Confessions, having moved, as Van Bavel has shown, in the years between A.D. 386 and 400, from emphasizing Christ's two natures to emphasizing his unity,[94] discussed his earlier λόγος-ἄνθρωπος emphasis from the viewpoint of the λόγος-σάρξ emphasis which "seriously reduces the fullness of Christ's humanity."[95] There is a subtle shift of accent to the tremendous condescension of 'mixture' of divinity with flesh,[96] "Godhead, weak because of its participation in our 'coats of skin.'" Augustine has explored the full range of orthodox Incarnational theology in these years between 386 and 400, even using formulas which an unsympathetic reviewer can easily find heretical.

We will not handle Augustine's mature Incarnational theory with the thoroughness and precision with which it has been analyzed by Van Bavel, Fortin, Newton, and others.[97] Our purposes here will be satisfied by a description which selects the basic developmental characteristics since what we are trying to demonstrate is that Augustine found it to be of the first importance to develop an Incarnational understanding and explanation. He struggled over it, going the full range from preconversion Photinianism to an extreme Alexandrian position, and it was not until A.D. 411-412 that Augustine developed a formula with which he was content. In this final formula, several characteristics appear which adumbrate the Chalcedonian formula.[98] We will discuss these characteristics under two categories: (1) Use of the analogy of the union of body and soul in human beings, and (2) Development of the metaphysical significance of the idea of persona.

There is an urgency in Augustine's work on the Incarnation, an urgency which occurs neither in the earlier patristic authors nor in the philosophers.[99] Augustine was the first of the fathers to recognize the full conceptual difficulty of the Incarnation because it was only in Augustine that the Stoicism of the earlier fathers and the Platonism of Plotinus and Porphyry came to full rational consciousness, and, therefore consciousness of conflict. This could have occurred with Victorinus or Ambrose in whom the Latin tradition and Plotinian philosophy came together; it did not emerge as a rational conflict in Victorinus because, excited with the possibility of illuminating Christianity with Platonism, he could not acknowledge the counter-indications, the fundamental conflict. Ambrose, on the other hand, was content to "affirm without understanding" because his concerns were predominantly ethical, political, pragmatic. But Augustine, sensitized from his youth to the fact that "one wry principle in the mind is of infinite consequence,"[100] was committed to the careful integration of his thought.

> But there are some who request an explanation of how God is joined to man so as to become the single person of Christ, as if they themselves could

> explain something that happens every day, namely how the soul is joined to the body so as to form the single person of a man.[101]

There is no doubt that Augustine's idea of the relation of body and soul is intimately linked with his understanding of the Incarnation. For Augustine, the conceptual understanding of a dogma must begin with experience. The most intimate and pre-conscious 'experience' of the human being, that of incarnation, is the paradigm of the Incarnation of the Word; in fact, as he explains in _Epistula_ CXXXVII, quoted above, the human composite is, on the conceptual level, the more difficult to understand since it involves a spiritual and a corporeal substance, while the Incarnation involves a unity of two spiritual substances, the soul of Christ and the Godhead. Earlier patristic authors had also used the analogy of physical union; indeed, Fortin finds that "the most popular analogy for the union of two natures employed by the fathers was that of union of body and soul in man."[102] Augustine adopts also the earlier fathers' concern to specify the limits of the analogy, to emphasize the uniqueness of the Incarnation.[103] But his use of the analogy, although reflecting the earlier fathers' 'union of predominance' theme,[104] has an important new dimension: Augustine was the "first Latin father to use the hypostatic union theory and its associated analogies to support the Incarnation."[105] Only circa A.D. 412, in _Epistula_ CXXXVII, does Augustine come to use this analogy with confidence; it has now been corrected by a richer conept of 'person.'

Grillmeier, Van Bavel, and others have shown in detail that the term _persona_ appears for the first time in _De agone Christiano_.[106] It was only after A.D. 400, and not with predictable consistency until circa 411 that _una persona_ is used by Augustine to define both distinctness of natures in Christ and unity of person.[107] The meaning of person in the sense of a unified complex is attested by other, more traditional supporting expressions: _idem_, _ipse_, _idem ipse_, _simul cum_, _totus_, _unus_.[108] Augustine has come to this understanding by making a pivotal distinction between _nature_ and _person_. The first clear expression of this occurs in _De Trinitate_ VII.6.11, written approximately A.D. 410-412: "Nature is something which is had in common, person, on the other hand is something 'aliquid singulare atque individum.'"[109] That two 'natures' can unite to form a single person is experientially available from our human condition. Beginning with _Epistula_ CXXXVII, the analogy of physical union takes on new appropriateness and significance, both for Augustine's idea of the union of body and soul in the human being and for Incarnational theory. It is largely this enriched understanding of the Incarnation which allows Augustine to affirm the unity of body and soul with a vigor unknown in the Dialogues.[110] As we have seen, Augustine was able to differentiate Christ's two natures from his earliest Christian writings; but the unity remained problematic until he applied the hypostatic union theory to the Incarnation. As Fortin points out, Gilson's statement that Augustine's theory of the soul owes nothing to the Incarnation is a misunderstanding.[111]

Yet it is apparent that Augustine has taken his understanding of the Incarnation directly from Neoplatonic doctrine. In _Epistula_ CXXXVII, responding to the pagan Volusianus, Augustine gives a clear description of the distinction in unity of the Incarnation; "it was Augustine's stated apologetic method to use a theory adopted by pagan philosophers in his apologetic works. . . in a letter written to Marcellinus immediately after _Epistula_ CXXXVII, he stated it was his intention to use authorities which the pagans would recognize."[112] In so using the Neoplatonic doctrine of _unio inconfusa_,[113] Augustine found a particularly happy solution to his long-time frustration.[114] Augustine continued to use the soul and body analogy and the _una persona_ formula in his major writings on the Incarnation.[115] The explanation always takes the form of describing a _unio inconfusa_, as it does in _Epistula_ CXXXVII.2:

> For as the soul makes use of the body in a single person to form a man, so God makes use of man in a single Person to form Christ. In the former person there is a mingling of soul and body; in the latter Person there is a mingling of God and man; but the hearer must abstract from the property of material substance by which two liquids are usually so mingled that neither retains its special character, although among such substances light mingled with air remains unchanged. Therefore, the person of man is a mingling of soul and body, but the Person of Christ is a mingling of God and man, for, when the Word of God is joined to a soul which has a body, it takes on both the soul

> and the body at once. The one process happens daily in order to beget men; the other happened once to set men free.[116]

But Augustine's work on the Incarnation was not finished, although it had achieved an important and permanent component with his full understanding of persona. The Pelagian controversy, beginning circa A.D. 411, prompted Augustine to deepen his understanding of the Incarnation. The later emphases are in the direction of (1) further work on articulating the nature of the union of the two natures in Christ, and (2) stressing the human component in Christ. Augustine has come full circle conceptually in the later emphasis, but with a major difference: human beings can fully identify with the humanity of Christ now that the unity of his two natures is articulated. It is only on the basis of the full conscious articulation of real distinctions that a true unity can be grasped. The enriched sense of mixtura in the later Augustine[117] is highly significant; no longer reflecting the classical uneasiness with 'mixture,' Augustine is free to image the conjunction of God and human in Christ as the highest activity;[118] the unity of Christ is no longer imaged statically as a 'watering down' of the human nature by the God nature, but as a summit, an extreme of achievement and value,[119] a 'mixture' in which human nature is immeasurably enriched. The assumption of human nature by the divine Word means that human nature is infinitely valuable; Incarnation is then truly the basis for the redemption of the whole human being, not just the 'highest part.' It is no longer only the Godlike and beautiful in human beings that is salvaged out of the clutter and inertia of the body, but the whole experience of human being.[120]

Augustine also expanded his idea of the significance of the Incarnation in the course of the Pelagian controversy; he came to identify the unique grace of Christ with the Incarnation.[121] The Incarnation is the intimate avenue of grace toward all mankind; the Incarnation is grace. The 'Doctor of Grace' has identified the union of two natures in Christ in all its concreteness as the source of the hope of the human being.[122] The 'in-fleshness' of Christ becomes the basis of the later Augustine's emphasis and celebration of Christ's full humanity.

The human soul of Christ is the locus of the cohesion of the two natures and is the *sine qua non* of their unity.[123]

> Nor should our faith be lessened by any reference to 'a woman's internal organs,' as if it might appear that we must reject any such generation of our Lord, because sordid people think that sordid. . . . Those who think this ought to observe that the rays of the sun . . . are poured over evil-smelling drains and other horrible things and do their natural work there without being made foul by any contamination, those visible, whose visible light is by nature more closely related to visible filth. How much less could the Word of God, who is neither visible nor corporeal, have been polluted by the body of a woman when he assumed human flesh along with a human soul and spirit, within which the majesty of the Word was hidden away from the weakness of the human body?[124]

Augustine never ceases to underline the humanity of Christ as the *condition* of our redemption.[125] Even after the Resurrection Christ's corporeality will be preserved.[126] The earlier fathers' 'union of predominance' emphasis has been importantly modified by this focus on the humanity of Christ. Against Wolfson's statement that "we may assume that it is 'predominance' that Augustine had in mind when . . . he says that 'man was united, and in some sense commixed (commixtus) with the Word of God so as to be one person,'" quoting *De Trinitate* IV.20.30, we should notice that the mere semantic occurrence of a word, 'mixture,' does not guarantee the identity of meaning; rather, the word has taken a very different connotation from its use in the early Augustine, due to his work on the Incarnation. That Augustine had become thoroughly acclimated to the notion of 'mixture' is substantiated in his coming to see mixture as characteristic, and not necessarily intrinsically negative, of the Church, the '*permixtum* body' of Christ; the citizens' allegiance to the *civitas terrena* or the *civitas Dei* also displays an element of "unpredictable mixture."[127] This different understanding of mixture as unity is also reflected in Augustine's view of the sacraments as developed in the Donatist controversy; it is the unity of Word and element that makes the sacrament of the Eucharist: "Take away the Word, and what is water except water? Add the Word to the element and the Sacrament is made, and even itself becomes the visible Word."[128]

Augustine's examined, articulated view of the Incarnation had the most direct and immediate bearing on his view of the unity of body and soul in man. Couturier points out that one of Augustine's major differences from the Platonists is his mature teaching that a 'natural appetite' attaches body and soul;[129] their separation at death is a 'tearing.'[130] The strong image of De civitate Dei XV[131] of the body as 'spouse' of the soul[132] is in marked contrast to his early unoriginal metaphors of body as 'snare' and 'cage.'[133] That this major reworking of values is the direct result of his work on the Incarnation is attested by the fact that his expositions of the relationship of body and soul occur in the mature and later works in passages in which he describes the Incarnation. It was his work on Incarnation that effected the reevaluation of the body; although his method begins with a philosophical understanding of body and soul, it is only because of being forced as a Christian thinker to deal with the Incarnation that his view of the meaning and value of the body is altered. As God and man constitute in Christ a persona, a unity of activity, so body and soul in man constitute an integration of being and activity, a person.

CHAPTER V

AUGUSTINE'S UNDERSTANDING OF RESURRECTION OF THE BODY: CASSICIACUM TO *DE CIVITATE DEI* XXII

> "Sed hoc interest, quia ista caro resurget, ista ipsa quae sepelitur, quae moritur; ista quae videtur, quae palpitur . . . "
>
> --*Sermo* CCLXIV.6

The dogma of the resurrection of the body was a compelling invitation to include the body in a more comprehensive understanding of human integrity than had been achieved by pagan thought. Yet Christians of Augustine's time had almost as much trouble with the dogma as did the educated pagans to whom *De Civitate Dei* is addressed.[1] C. N. Cochrane and others have explored the philosophical implications of this integration of personality; what has been less acknowledged and explored is that Augustine himself began his career as a Christian priest and author with an idea of immortality of the soul which excludes resurrection of the body.[2] Yet Augustine's theology of the resurrection of the body came to be what one of his biographers has called "a central preoccupation" in his old age,[3] tremendously enriched by a life-long struggle to grasp its essential meaning.[4] Once again our method will be to document the development of this theology of the bodily resurrection in three periods, the early writings before about A.D. 393, the mature writings from the time of his ordination as a bishop, and finally, the period of his old age from about A.D. 418 to his death.

But first, in order to grasp the dimensions of the philosophical and theological tradition which formulated the questions to which Augustine addressed himself, a brief summary of Judaic, philosophical, Scriptural, and early Christian traditions before Augustine's time will be given.

In the Old Testament, the body participates with the soul in very close association in the higher activities. There is no rationale offered for resurrection of the flesh; it is presented as "a mystery dependent on God's wishes."[5] Death is natural; only premature death is startling and disconcerting. The anthropological model is that of the animated body; the soul's function is to animate the body with whom it is integrated. It loses its own reality and true nature when it ceases to animate the body.[6] The doctrine of a general resurrection is late and limited to certain circles, although earlier texts do not exclude the possibility.[7] Jesus did not explicitly teach a general resurrection,[8] but the Pharisees affirmed a resurrection of the just. As a Pharisee, Paul awaited the resurrection of the body as he later would as a Christian. His first letter to the Corinthians was written to correct exactly those gnostic tendencies in the Corinthian Church which rejected resurrection of the body. "Why," the Corinthians had asked, "having been liberated from the body, would we want to be reunited with that carcass?"[9] I Corinthians 15, the chapter from which Augustine "drew his entire theology of the resurrection,"[10] is Paul's grand defense and description of the bodily resurrection.[11]

Except for the Epicureans, all the dogmatic philosophers of the Hellenistic and Roman worlds included survival--more or less personal and prolonged--of 'the most elevated part of man,' conceived by each system in its own way, but "always by opposition to the body."[12] "The resurrection of the flesh . . . is not the complement of the immortality of the soul, but its contradiction."[13] For the Stoics, reported by Tertullian to hold that the soul has a limited immortality and is corporeal, the journey of the soul after death was admittedly difficult or impossible to conceptualize;[14] Tertullian lists several opinions concerning it: some said that the soul exists until the next universal conflagration; some said that only the souls of sages survive. Panaetius rejected the immortality of the soul entirely, holding that the soul does not survive the death of the body, and "no Stoic postulated unlimited survival or immortality."[15] Tertullian emphasized that no one had ever taught the resurrection of the flesh.[16]

However, it may be that the familiar emphasis of scholars on the dogma of the bodily resurrection as a startling innovation needs to be significantly modified. J. M. C. Toynbee has documented, from funerary inscriptions and accoutrements, a belief current during the late Republic and throughout the Empire, in "the survival after death of personal individuality." Although current ideas as to the location and structure of the other world were "confused and conflicting . . . views on the nature of the life that awaited the soul beyond the grave were in the main optimistic."[17] It is a large step, to be sure, from belief in the survival of "personal individuality" to belief in resurrection of the body, but the survival of a center of personal consciousness implies--and perhaps even requires--a 'body' of some sort.[18] In addition, in support of this argument for a "significant strengthening of emphasis" on the survival of individual personality, Toynbee cites the gradual abandonment of the practice of cremation, standard until the second century A.D., "too early to be due to Christian influences." By the second century, the art of sarcophagus carving began to indicate a rise in inhumation which "by the middle of the third century had won its way throughout the provinces."[19] It is possible that this change in consciousness was an important precursor for the belief in the resurrection of the body.

Plato's doctrine of immortality of the soul is notoriously inconsistent,[20] ranging from the implication in the _Phaedo_ and the _Republic_ that, since the soul has no parts, all of it must be immortal,[21] to the _Timaeus_ in which the two lower parts of the soul are mortal so that only the rational part would survive. Plotinus, attempting to formulate a coherent and systematic doctrine, had to infer and innovate this point. A. N. M. Rich writes:

> Does the irrational soul perish with the body? Plotnius answers this question in the negative. When the body is discarded, he says, "all powers merge into one soul" (IV.9.3). Thus, desire, feeling, and the power of sensation lose their specific character when their raison d'être has gone, and like the discursive faculty, become absorbed into the higher phase of the soul, that has always held itself aloof from the body. Even the φυτικόν, the source of physical life, survives bodily death. For a brief time it may actually linger within the body after death has occurred; this is evident from the fact that hair and nails may continue to grow upon a corpse (IV.4.29). But eventually it abandons all connection with that particular organism and returns to its source

> in the World Soul, only to re-emerge as the animating source in some other individual.[22]

Yet the doctrine of the immortality of the soul is ancillary for Plotinus as for Plato; ultimately it is not a question of the survival of the whole human being, but only of the rational part which subsumes the rest of the person. In Ennead III.6.6, the only passage in which he uses the word ανάστασις, Plotinus clarifies the point that the body has no real share in the 'spiritual redressment'[23] of the person: ". . . the true awakening is a true getting up from the body, not with the body.[24]

Yet we must be careful not to overemphasize Plotinus' 'contempt' for the body; nowhere does he suggest that the vision of the One after death is "intrinsically different from or superior to that attainable in this life, or that the soul when it is out of the cycle of reincarnation has greater purity or capacity of vision than when it is in it."[25] This lack of extolling the disembodied state has the effect of drastically curtailing 'otherworldliness' in Plotinus; we will explore this more fully in the context of examining Augustine's ideas.

Armstrong's suggestion of a popular cultural influence on Neoplatonism is important here:

> The pagan Neoplatonists, like other men of their time, were affected by that cosmic religiosity which saw the divinity far more perfectly manifested in (if not identified with) the Upper Cosmos above the moon than in the sublunary world, which glorified heavenly bodies and despised earthly ones, and hoped for some kind of return to the visible heavens after death. The Christian fiercely rejected the idea of the divinity of the Upper Cosmos and of the sun, moon and stars, but found it all too easy to translate the opposition of the celestial and earthly bodies into the theological language of their own doctrine of the resurrection. St. Augustine clearly saw a connection between the two doctrines.[26]

The lingering psychological effects of the comparison of earthly bodies with all their enormities and deformities with the apparently changeless perfection of the heavenly bodies, may have been much stronger in the popular mind than we might guess when dealing only with the doctrines of the great Neoplatonic teachers.[27]

There is no evidence that Plotinus ever discussed the Christian dogma of the bodily resurrection, but Porphyry did, and it is his interpretation and rejection of this dogma which Augustine will argue against in *De Civitate Dei*. Porphyry's main objections to Christianity, according to Augustine, were to the Incarnation and the Resurrection. In fact, Augustine states twice in *De Civitate Dei* X.29 that Porphyry's "omne corpus fugiendum" was formulated "precisely to counteract the Christian teaching of the resurrection."[28] The *Philosophy from Oracles*, described by Augustine under the title *De regressu animae*,

> denied the resurrection of all bodies as absurd. It taught that for beatitude in heaven, the soul must be separated from all bodies whatsoever: there could be no question of the soul's returning to its original body in any condition. It admitted that Christ's soul was immortal and in heaven, a lot which could be possessed by any human. But the body of Christ and all other bodies must be left behind at death to perish and dissolve. . . .[29]

Augustine taxes Porphyry with inconsistency for his adage "omne corpus fugiendum" since the pagan Platonists believed in astral or celestial bodies.[30] To Porphyry, however, several aspects of the Christian dogma seemed crudely materialistic.

In short, gnostics and philosophers shared, for different reasons, an opposition to the Christian belief in the resurrection of the body. For the Manichaeans, the body is "inherently damned. . . . Obviously there could be no question of a redemption or resurrection of the body."[31] "The crucial point of divorce between pagan thought and Christian dogma, even though pagan thought agreed on the immortality of the soul, was the resurrection of the body. No one in the Greco-Roman world had ever believed in such a resurrection."[32]

Nygren has called attention to the fact that the dogma of the resurrection of the flesh "plays a far greater part in the apologists than in primitive Christianity, and the reason is undoubtedly their reaction against the Hellenistic doctrines of salvation"[33] in which, as Porphyry faithfully reflects, the immortality of the soul is set in opposition and contrast to the resurrection of the body. We will now look at the patristic tradition prior to Augustine in order to set a context for Augustine's idea of the resurrection.

Although some scholars have distinguished a 'Greek tradition' and a 'theological' or Latin tradition concerning the nature of the resurrection body of Christ, Charles Journet has argued that it is inaccurate to make such a distinction in which in the Latin tradition the resurrection body of Christ was a fleshly but transformed body, while the Greek fathers emphasized the absorption of Jesus' resurrected body in a spiritual glory.[34] He demonstrates that we have unambiguous statements from the earliest fathers--Clement of Rome, Ignatius, and Polycarp--as to the substantiality of the resurrected body of Christ and of human beings, and that in fact many of these statements occur in the context of combatting the spiritualist emphasis of the docetists.[35] In the Apologists, the same insistence continues: "It is said that only the soul is immortal," Tatian wrote; "I say that the flesh is also."[36] Athenagoras, in his treatise _De resurrectione mortis_, is explicit in insisting that it is the whole human being which has received life, not the soul alone, and thus it must be the whole human being that will be resurrected:

> We look to the resurrection, putting up with the dissolution of the body as consequent upon a life that is involved in needs and decay, and we hope for permanence in incorruption after this life.[37]

One of the major objections brought to the dogma of the bodily resurrection was the case of those whose bodies have been dismembered or eaten by wild beasts.[38] The way this question was handled serves to underscore the fathers'--even the Greek fathers'--almost embarrassingly literal image of the resurrection. We do not find the spiritualist view, attributed by Maurice Pontet and others to the Greeks,[39] except in Origen.

It would be of the highest interest to be able to read Origen's now lost early work on the resurrection. The controversy over what Origen actually taught continues to occupy scholars today as it did in the late fourth century.[40] It will be impossible to clarify here beyond the point that these scholars have agreed to disagree. However, it seems certain that some unique features of Origen's teaching place his views outside the traditional teachings of the fathers on resurrection of the body.[41] Origen criticized several points on which the other fathers are in agreement; for example, their appeal to divine omnipotence as a rationale for the resurrection,[42] their argument that Jesus' resurrection provides a paradigm and 'earnest' for each person's resurrection,[43] and the defense of the resurrection of people eaten by wild beasts in which the other fathers revealed their images of the resurrection body as complete with members and interior and exterior parts. Origen uses this example to illustrate the impossibility of such a tangible body; for him, people eaten by wild beasts become part of the beast![44] Rather, the form (εῖδος) of the body is what is resurrected. The debate of scholars has to do with the relative degree of abstract spirituality or concrete physicality intended by Origen in this formula. The debate is fascinating--but not edifying--and we cannot follow it here.[45] Origen's teaching[46] is apparently that within the mortal corruptible body there is a latent 'germ' which develops into a spiritual or astral body, a λόγος σπέρματικος. This spiritual body is of the same nature as the physical body and comes from the same source, which makes possible an affirmation of their identity.[47]

Journet concludes his analysis of Origen's view of the resurrection: "It is impossible to deny a deviation from the former doctrine of the Fathers."[48] But is Origen's influence appreciable on the fathers after his time? We find in Methodius, in Hilary, and in Epiphanius the strongest statements concerning the identity of the mortal body with the resurrection body.[49] The Cappadocian fathers, perhaps the most strongly influenced by Origen's theology, although envisioning the resurrection body as "spiritual" in that it is perfectly integrated with the soul, still indicate that they do not image this spiritualization of the body as a negation of its full humanity but indeed as an infinite amplification of this humanity. Augustine's contemporary, Gregory of Nyssa, taught that "the soul retrieves in the resurrection not only a true body, but also the material elements themselves which constitute its own body."[50] Certainly one sees in this statement, as Journet says, not an excess of spiritualism, "but on the contrary, an excessive realism."[51] John Chrysostom and John of

Damascus, the last of the Greek fathers, in dealing with I Corinthians 15:44, are careful to emphasize that it is not the total spiritualization of the body that Paul teaches, but that "the spirit will always remain in the flesh of the righteous."[52] It seems that the Greek fathers have been too hastily seen as continuing Origen's spiritualist emphasis in the area of their views on the resurrection body.[53] I agree with Journet in seeing here only one tradition of the fathers, and Origen's view as deviant.

The Latin fathers after Origen are in agreement with the Greek fathers in their insistence on three points concerning the resurrection: the fact of the resurrection, the universality of the resurrection, and the identity of the resurrection body.[54] Jerome's changing views on the nature of the resurrection body reflect his early Origenist preoccupation and his later repudiation of Origen. Although he may have exaggerated Origen's view, his early statements teach the total spiritualization of the body and the disappearance of the sexes in the resurrection.[55] After his repudiation of Origen in A.D. 394, he taught, in very graphic imagery, the identity of the resurrection body with the earthly body.[56] Ambrose also underscores the material reality of the resurrection body, despite its transformation.[57]

Thus we begin our exploration of Augustine's view of the resurrection in the context of an unambiguous tradition, colored only slightly by Origen's differing view. There seems on this question to be a conscious correction for this spiritualist view in exactly the Greek authors in which we would most expect to find agreement with Origen.

i

Augustine's first mention of the bodily resurrection occurs in *De quantitate animae* 76, written shortly after his return from Cassiciacum. He there declares the resurrection of "naturae huius corporeae" to be "as certain as the rising of the sun," but several lines further in the same passage, he describes death as "the sheer flight and escape from this body, . . . now yearned for as the greatest boon." We have evidence here, as in the regular references to death in the Cassiciacum dialogues as a liberation from the body, that Augustine was affirming a Christian doctrine but without, as O'Connell says, being able to offer a "shred of understanding" of it.[58] Rather, he affirms the bodily resurrection in the face of his own tendency to Neoplatonic ambivalence or dualistic repudiation of the body.

We will examine two of Augustine's ideas concerning the resurrection of the body in this early period until A.D. 393 which were to undergo significant change in the mature writings. Both of these ideas imply and require the assumption of the immortality of the soul and demonstrate Augustine's eagerness to interpret the Christian dogma of the bodily resurrection in a way which is congruent with the philosophers' idea of the immortality of the soul. Three early texts borrow Plato's argument for immortality of the soul in the Phaedo;[59] Augustine alters the argument to conform to the Christian idea of God as Creator and Preserver of the soul, but there is no mention in these passages of the body as participant in the soul's eternal life. The ideas with which Augustine supports his idea of the immortality of the soul are (1) that the vision of God could be complete in this life, and (2) that concrete human physicality could have no part in the resurrection. We will examine these in turn.

Peter Brown has written a masterful chapter in his biography, Augustine of Hippo, describing Augustine's change, in the first decade of his conversion, from the idea, common in late classical thought, that the "perfect life" is possible on this earth for the philosopher-saint.

> When Augustine, therefore, spoke of the quality of life achieved by his heroes, the Apostles, we can see exactly what he was hoping for himself: "'Blessed are the peacemakers.' For those are peacemakers in themselves, who, in conquering and subjecting to reason . . . all the motions of their souls and having their carnal desires tamed, have become, in themselves, a Kingdom of God. . . . They enjoy the peace which is given on earth to men of good-will . . . the life of the consummate and perfect man of wisdom. . . . All this can reach fulfillment in this present life, as we believe it was reached by the Apostles."[60]

The causes of this change are very carefully analyzed in the chapter "The Lost Future," and I will refer to them here only in direct connection with Augustine's changing valuation of the resurrection of the body. For a person who thinks that the complete vision of God is attainable in this life, the immortality of the soul is nothing but a continuation of this spiritual life. We have seen this affirmation of the possibilities of the present life in Plotinus.[61] And Augustine's dialogues at Cassiciacum show that he thought this goal was attainable "not only for a moment here and there, but in a semipermanent way."[62]

Curiously, it is in De quantitate animae XXIII.76, the very passage in which the bodily resurrection is mentioned for the first time, that Augustine outlines in detail the method of "arriving at the Vision" of the Supreme Good. Augustine strongly affirms the bodily resurrection, using a traditional metaphor:

> We shall also see that this corporeal nature, in obedience to the divine law, undergoes so many changes and vicissitudes that we may hold even the resurrection of the body (which some believe too late; others not at all) to be so certain that the rising of the sun, after it has gone down, is not more certain to us.[63]

Yet the resurrection of the body functions in the passage to argue toward a strange conclusion--one with which we are familiar from the later Stoics, from Plotinus, and, most immediately, from Ambrose:

> Then death, which was an object of fear and an obstacle to the soul's fullest union with the full truth, death, namely, the sheer flight and escape from this body, is now yearned for as the greatest boon.[64]

There is no continuity between our bodily experience and our anticipation of the resurrection of the body. Although the image Augustine uses is drawn from experience, indeed from the most fundamental and universal experience,[65] Augustine at this time does not see or describe any connection between our mortal bodies and resurrection bodies. His thought is ambiguous, if not contradictory; like Plotinus he values the mortal body implicitly in that it is the condition in which the complete vision can occur; yet when he describes the permanent perfection of the vision, he unconsciously borrows Porphyry's formula: "ab hoc corpore omnimoda fuga et elapsio."[66] There is no real integration of the body in Augustine's description of the experience of the highest human value. The paratactic formula so commonly used in the mature writings to connect our experience: *nunc* . . . *tunc* . . ., does not appear here.[67] We have rather a mutual contamination of present and future, due to Augustine's failure to integrate the role of the body.

It is in *De Genesi ad litteram* that Augustine first seriously considers the relation of the *corpus animale* to the *corpus spirituale*. Adam, he writes, had a "pristine animal body,"[68] but it is not to this sort of body that we will be changed in the resurrection, but to a spiritual body, "a spiritual body into which Adam had not yet been changed, but was to be changed, if he had not in sinning deserved death also of his animalic body."[69] In this period, "Augustine applied a Christian's *renovatio in melius* only to his ultimate resurrection and not to this life on earth." What is possible now, however, is that "we are being renewed to the image of the Creator, though not according to our body, but *spiritu mentios nostrae*."[70] We can see Augustine's idea here in process of change; he is sorting his ideas of the possibilities for this life and for the resurrection. We find the formula *nunc* . . . *tunc* . . . for the first time in *Contra Faustum Manichaeum* in A.D. 398:

> There is *now* a restoration of the inner man, when it is renewed after the image of its Creator, in putting off unrighteousness, that is, the old man. *Then*, however, when that which has been sown an animal body shall rise a spiritual body, the outer man too shall gain the value of a participant in the heavenly . . .[71]

A continuity of experience is posited in this formula; the terms are antithetical, but their parallelism implies an experiential relationship such as St. Paul describes in I Corinthians 13:12: "We see now through a shadowy mirror; then, however, face to face." The contrast assumes a continuity. We will discuss Augustine's continuing development in his idea of the possibilities *nunc* and *tunc* in the section on his mature works. It is sufficient here to demonstrate a contrast between the works before A.D. 393, in which the bodily resurrection is affirmed but not related to our present experience because (1) it need not be longed for since the "vision" is available in this life, and (2) we have no experience of physical being which in any way adumbrates or images the resurrection body, and the works of a short time later in which a relationship between our experience nunc and tunc is assumed. Ten years after the Cassiciacum dialogues, Augustine wrote:

> Whoever thinks that in this mortal life a man may so disperse the mists of bodily and carnal imaginings as to possess the unclouded light of changeless truth, and to cleave to it with the unswerving constancy of a spirit wholly estranged from the common ways of life--he understands neither what he seeks, nor who he is that seeks it.[72]

The second idea of the early works on the bodily resurrection which we will examine is Augustine's reluctance to posit the participation of any concrete human physicality in the resurrection body. In De fide et symbolo, Augustine's address to a Council of the African Church in A.D. 393 while he was still a priest, he treats the resurrection of the body. His treatment is a skillful synthesis of philosophical and theological language which, most of the time, operates to complement and reinforce his thought.[73] Yet there is conflict at one significant point in Augustine's language, reflecting a corresponding ambivalence in his thought. He discusses, in IV.6, Verbum caro factum est.[74] The word 'flesh,' when used to describe Christ's earthly body, is acceptable to Augustine, but 'flesh' becomes pejorative when he describes the bodily resurrection, and he is at lengthy pains to eliminate it, using Paul's "Flesh and blood shall not inherit the kingdom of heaven" as the basis of his argument that an immutatio angelica stands between our fleshly experience and the resurrection, which is to be described accurately not as 'flesh' but as 'body.'[75] The confirmation for this interpretation of Augustine's argument in De fide et symbolo is Augustine's own correction of the passage in Retractationes I.16:

> But anyone who interprets this in such a way as to think that the earthly body as we have it now is so changed into a celestial body at the resurrection that there will be neither these members nor the substance of flesh, certainly, without a doubt, is to be reproved, admonished by the body of the Lord who, after the resurrection, appeared with the same members.

Nevertheless in the early Augustine, not only is the human flesh of our experience to have no part in the resurrection body but these bodies will have neither limbs nor bones.[76] An interesting example of Augustine's changing view of the concrete physicality of the resurrection body is his treatment of the question of whether the vision of God will be seen with the eyes of the body. A contemporary of Augustine, Synesius of Cyrene, A.D. 370-413, was ordained a Christian bishop in Alexandria without subscribing to the dogma of the resurrection of the body: ". . . his objections are still close to those of Celsus, for whom the Christians were men of flesh, not of the soul, who hoped for the resurrection of the body because of their pathetic belief that it would be necessary for them to have eyes in order to see God."[77] As late as Epistula XCII,[78] in which he calls the idea 'insane,' and in the Commonitarium ad Fortunatianus,[79] Augustine argues that "man will not see God in heaven with the eyes of his body."[80] But in De Civitate Dei XXII.29, Augustine's last word on the subject, he offers a lengthy discussion, concluding that although it is difficult, if not impossible, to support this suggestion by any passages in holy Scripture,

> it is possible, indeed most probable, that we shall then see the physical bodies of the new heaven and the new earth in such a fashion as to observe God in utter clarity and distinctness, seeing him present everywhere and governing the whole material scheme of things by means of the bodies we shall then inhabit and the bodies we shall see wherever we turn our eyes.[81]

The change in Augustine's view of the resurrection body occurs most dramatically in the course of the 390s, but his relevant statements continue to show the inconsistency which marks an incomplete integration of his theoretical understanding until quite late in his life. The change in his theoretical understanding occurs in connection with the disillusionment discussed above about the possibility of any immediate and lasting availability of the vision of God. The translation of Augustine's early experiences of momentary vision into a life-style had proved overwhelmingly difficult. But a more direct reason for his change--and here I think we are dealing with an essential change, not simply a development of emphasis--was his ongoing personal polemic against Manichaeism,[82] a polemic in which he was forced to study St. Paul's teaching on the resurrection in order to combat the Manichaean rejection of the doctrine of the resurrection of the body. In the reply to Faustus the

Manichaean,[83] he demonstrates the result of this study in a detailed exposition of I Corinthians 15. Faustus, himself an expositor of St. Paul, taught a docetist view of the Incarnation of Christ and denied both Christ's resurrection and that of human beings.[84] In answering Faustus' objections to the resurrection, Augustine cites Paul's "It is sown a natural body; it is raised a spiritual body. . . . But this I say, brethren, that flesh and blood cannot inherit the kingdom of God." We have seen how he dealt with this text in *De fide et symbolo*; in the approximately five years which have elapsed between these works, Augustine has developed a significantly different interpretation. His method in the reply to Faustus is to demonstrate Paul's concern that his words not be interpreted to mean that "it is not the bodily substance" which will enter into the resurrection of the just. He shows that each new phase of Paul's argument anticipates precisely Faustus' docetic objections--and, although he does not mention it--his own earlier spiritualization of the resurrection.

> And in case anyone should still suppose that it is not what is buried that is to rise again but that it is as if one garment were laid aside and a better one taken instead, he proceeds to show distinctly that the same body will be changed for the better, as the garments of Christ on the Mount were not displaced but transfigured. . . . And if it should be said that it is not as regards our mortal and corruptible body, but as regards our soul, that we are to be changed, it should be observed that the apostle is not speaking of the soul, but of the body.[85]

The difference in Augustine's treatment of the same passage on these two occasions is more than one of altered emphasis due to different audiences--the one, *De fide et symbolo*, to priests and bishops of the African Church who presumably did not need to be instructed in the fundamentals of the faith, the other to a strong rival sect. This will account for differences of tone and emphases of content; but more than that is apparent here. In fact, Augustine will continue to quote this text, I Corinthians 15:30, at least twenty-five times in commentaries on the Creed. His principal argument is furnished by Luke 24:39: "See my hands and my feet. . . ."[86] He never returned to his original interpretation of the text.

To conclude this discussion of Augustine's early idea of the resurrection body, we will look briefly at the continuities of his teaching. Two fundamental tenets remain strong from his earliest to his last description of the resurrection body: Augustine always viewed the resurrection of the body as the cornerstone of the Christian faith; and, from the beginning of his Christian teaching, he taught that Christ's resurrection body is the paradigm and guarantee of that of each human being.

The dogma of the resurrection of the body was understood by the early Church to be an irreducible article of Christian faith. "It is noteworthy that this article is not missing from any one of the ancient versions of the Creed that have come down to us." Augustine affirms this dogma from the beginning, treats it emphatically from _De fide et symbolo_ on, and by A.D. 398 he offers in the _Contra Faustum Manichaeum_ an understanding of it based strongly on I Corinthians 15.[87]

In the early _Sermo_ XXII.10.10, Augustine wrote: "Since that flesh which rose again and, restored to life, ascended into heaven, received resurrection and eternal life, this too is promised to us."[88] This is by no means a strong theme in the early period;[89] yet it is in Augustine's mind as the validation of the belief in the bodily resurrection. _De fide et symbolo_ presents a lack of understanding of it as a 'virtue.'

> But the question as to where and in what manner the Lord's body is in heaven, is one which it would be altogether overcurious (_curiosissimum_) and superfluous (_supervaceneum_) to ask. Only we must believe that it is in heaven. For it pertains not to our frailty to investigate the secret things of heaven, but it does pertain to our faith to hold elevated and honorable sentiments on the subject of the dignity of the Lord's body.[90]

But from the time of _Contra Faustum Manichaeum_ and _Contra Felicem Manichaeum_ (c. A.D. 398), the references to Christ's body as the _exemplum_ of the _resurrectio carnis_ increase, and show increasing significance in Augustine's thought.[91] Augustine began his career as a Christian teacher with a commitment to faith in the resurrection of the body; he believed in order to understand. Our exploration of his mature view will indicate Augustine's rich and profound understanding of the dogma of the _resurrectio carnis_.

ii

In Sermo CCXIII.9, Augustine addresses the basic discomfort of his congregation with the resurrection of the body: "Do not shudder at the resurrection of the body. See its good aspects; forget the evil. As a matter of fact, whatever bodily complaints there are now will not exist then."[92] The major rationale used by Augustine in the mature period to describe the nature and necessity of the resurrection body is that it will be the same body, truly a body and numerically identical. But also it will not be the same body because it will lack concupiscence and corruption. A. H. Armstrong suggests that resurrection of the body did not make as much difference as it should between Christian and Platonist attitudes to the body since "from the beginning the Christian tradition had stressed . . . the difference of the glorified resurrection body from the body as we know it in this life."[93] This objection cannot apply to Augustine; I will argue that, while Augustine treats carefully the difference of the resurrection body and the body as we know it, his emphasis is on their identity. Let us examine Augustine's idea of the difference and sameness of the resurrection by analyzing his method of understanding and expounding the resurrection of the body.

Augustine's method is a constant search for an image or images adequate to adumbrate the resurrection. As early as A.D. 386, he described the need for imagery with which to express and illuminate ideas:

> . . . it is a fact that anything made known by an allegorical expression inspires and delights us more, and is more esteemed by us than if it were most clearly stated in plain words. I believe that the emotions are enflamed more slowly as long as the soul is encircled by earthly things; but if it is directed to likenesses of corporeal things which are pictured by these likenesses, it is invigorated, as it were, in the transition, and like the flame of a torch is made to burn more brightly by the motion, and is carried to rest by a glowing love.[94]

At least twenty years later the same method is described in the passage in De Trinitate XI.1.1, which concludes: ". . . if at any time we would endeavor to distinguish more aptly and intimate more clearly the inward spiritual things, we must take examples of similitudes from outward things pertaining to the body."[95]2 We have seen that Augustine's first mention of the resurrection of the body in *De quantitate animae* 76 uses the metaphor of the rising of the sun. In several passages he likens our flesh to the moon, which also dies and rises again.[96] Yet these images, although experiential, do not satisfy Augustine. It is difficult to pinpoint the moment at which the adequate--even perfect--metaphor came to him; it seems rather to have emerged as a growing awareness, intimately connected with his changing evaluation of the human body. Certainly by the time of *Sermones* CCXL through CCXLIII--between A.D. 418 and 420--Augustine has seen and developed the implications of the human body itself as the experiential metaphor for the resurrection body. His metaphor for the resurrection has moved from the distant analogy of the sun and the moon to the fundamental human experience of embodiment.

He is careful to explicate his metaphor. Augustine goes beyond Paul in insisting, even while he follows Paul's distinction between *corpus animale* and *corpus spirituale*, that the nature of the resurrection body will remain the same, "without a trace, however, of any remnant of corruption or clumsiness";[97] although it will become, in a sense, 'angelic,' it still remains a body.[98] We can project some rich expectations on the basis of the identity of the resurrection body with the earthly body, but the limitations of the metaphor must be underlined:

> If I were to say that the body would rise again to be hungry and thirsty, to be sick and to suffer, to be subject to corruption, you would be right in refusing to believe me. . . . The flesh will rise incorruptible; the flesh will rise without defect, without blemish, without mortality, without burden, and without weight. What now brings pain to you will then be your glory.[99]

The resurrection will eliminate the corruptibility of the body and bring about its '*sanitas perfecta*.'[100] It is not the body of our experience in that it will not suffer from any of the lengthy list of dangers and diseases in *De civitate Dei* XXII. Yet it is on the basis of our present bodily experience that we can begin to image the life of the resurrection. Augustine's extrapolation of the *felicitas* of the resurrection, which has become very concrete by Book XXII of _De civitate Dei_, is clearly based on experience: "We have some experience of this situation in the distorted condition of our state of punishment."[101]

Even the 'place' of this eternal enjoyment of God and each other is for Augustine, to a high degree, experiential. Although "Augustine was not the first of the fathers to teach the optimistic view that the present world will continue after the conflagration and will be transformed into the new heavens and the new earth, the final setting for man's eternal enjoyment of God,"[102] it is significant that Augustine describes the transformation of the cosmos "in terminology identical with that employed for the resurrection of the body," and explicitly associates them. "In each case the substance or nature remains. The old corruptible qualities are replaced by new, incorruptible ones. There is a change for the better."[103]

Let us look more closely at Augustine's commitment to remaining close to experience in his description of the resurrection of the body. In a long excursus leading to a discussion on the resurrection of the body in _De civitate Dei_ XXI.7 to XXII.4, Augustine is at great pains to support his argument that, although the resurrection is ultimately non-experiential, it is supported on all sides by experience. The argument is specifically directed against 'the rationalists'--those who rely on reason alone--and Augustine's entire method is to direct attention to the facts of observation and experience.[104] Reason, operating _in vacuo_, can indeed posit absolute and final death, but it is totally contradictory to the facts of experience which attest, on every hand, the irruption of life and miracle. Miracles are essentially "not contrary to nature, but contrary to what is known of nature"; they demonstrate "that God is to do what he prophesied he would do with the bodies of the dead, with no difficulty to hinder him, no law of nature to debar him from so doing."[105] In addition, God has accomplished the embodiment of human souls--which Augustine still characterizes as "utterly amazing and beyond our powers of comprehension"[106]--and the daily miracle of an orderly universe,[107] in order to exhibit to human sense the ubiquity of the marvelous: "In fact, many miracles have occurred, as we cannot deny, to testify to that one supreme miracle of salvation, the miracle of Christ's ascension into heaven in the flesh in which he rose from the dead."[108] Thus miracles are experiential; the promised miracle of the resurrection of the body, then, should not utterly boggle the mind.

Yet there is an irreducibly nonexperiential component in the Christian's hope of the resurrection of the body. In the *De Genesi contra Manichaeos*, Augustine had given Adam a 'spiritual body'; but by the time of the *De Genesi ad litteram* VI.19, he writes that Adam was created in a *corpus animale* and, as a paradigm for all men, would be changed in the resurrection not merely into his pristine state, but *in melius*:[109] "We shall be renewed from the oldness of sin not into the pristine animalic body in which Adam was, but into a better one, that is to say, into a spiritual body."[110] *Corpus animale* is a body "moved by and subject to a human soul." Just so, "*corpus spirituale* does not 'become a spirit,' but is directed and penetrated by *spiritus*."[111] There is a *concordia carnis et spiritus*[112] which is the distinctive characteristic of the resurrection body:

> They have not been called 'spiritual' because they will be spirits, not bodies. . . . Why, then, is it called a spiritual body, my dearly beloved, except because it will obey the direction of the spirit? Nothing in yourself will be at variance with yourself; nothing in yourself will rebel against yourself.[113]

In short, the resurrection body will cease to be a hindrance to the soul in the soul's quest for happiness.[114]

Augustine declaims a characteristic reluctance to speculate on the details of the life of the resurrection body.[115] Yet those of us who have studied Augustine have learned to expect a lengthy conjecture to follow just such a disclaimer! We are not to be disappointed in this case, any more than Augustine could disappoint the many correspondents of his time who brought to him the variety of hackneyed objections and difficulties which obsessed people's minds. One senses in Augustine's patient, but insistently hypothetical, answers to these questions[116] the generosity of a great mind putting itself at the service of real people in their intellectual perplexities.[117]

In order to help people image and anticipate the resurrection, Augustine consents to speculate a bit concerning the nature of the resurrection body: first, the resurrection body will have great beauty; indeed, certain parts of the body, such as men's beards, which even now have no ascertainable function and exist solely for beauty, will be retained, for the same reason, together with other members which now have a function--such as the sexual organs. All will be preserved and glorified, in spite of having no direct usefulness.[118] Secondly, the resurrection body will have a weightless agility:

> The bodies of the saints, then shall rise again free from any defect, from every blemish, as from all corruption, weight and impediment. For their ease of movement shall be as complete as their happiness.[119]

Thirdly, the life of the resurrection body will be active--"Does existing, seeing, loving, praising seem idleness to you?"[120]--but without labor. There will be a capacity for food, but no need for it.[121] The image which the mature Augustine paints of the life of the resurrection body indicates a dramatic reevaluation of the meaning and value of the human body:[122]

> There where the greatest peace will prevail, nothing will be unsightly, nothing inharmonious, nothing monstrous, nothing calculated to offend the eyes, but in all things God will be praised. For if now, in such frailty of the flesh and in such weak operation of our members, such great beauty of the body appears that it entices the passionate and stimulates the learned and the thoughtful to investigate it . . . . how much more beautiful will the body be there where there will be no passion, no corruption, no unsightly deformity, no miserable necessity, but, instead, unending eternity, beautiful truth, and the utmost happiness?[123]

We must now look more closely at the nonexperiential element in the resurrection of the body. Despite Augustine's speculation on the basis of 'minusing oneself' of corruption, pain, and distress, his image of the resurrection body requires finally a model; the resurrection body of Christ as reported in Scripture is paradigmatic. But it was not only Origen who argued for the uniqueness of Christ's physical resurrection;[124] Augustine lists this objection among current difficulties with viewing Christ's resurrection as a model or exemplar of that of all human beings:

> You say that Christ was resurrected, and on this basis you hope for the resurrection of the dead. . . . But it is only Christ who received permission to rise from the dead. . . . These people who dare to compare themselves with Christ believe that if Christ was resurrected, they will be also![125]

But Augustine insists that "the Lord furnished us an example in his own case so that we might know what to hope for at the end of the world in our own bodies."[126] It is Christ's voluntary participation in human flesh that Augustine cites as his rationale for Christ as paradigm; his works after *circa* A.D. 400 "underline, in very strong terms," the corporeality of Christ even after the Resurrection.[127] In answer to Consentius' question concerning "whether the Lord's body has bones and blood or other marks of flesh," Augustine quotes Luke 24:37-39, a passage which he will often use in this connection:

> I think . . . . that the body of the Lord is the same now in heaven as it was when he ascended into heaven. When his disciples doubted his Resurrection, as we read in the Gospel, and thought that what they saw was not a body but a spirit, He said to them: "See my hands and my feet; handle and see; for a spirit hath not flesh and bones as you see me to have."[128]

This point is important to Augustine: Christ's solidarity with the Christian in participation in the experience of embodiment does not end with his earthly body, but persists as a model and guarantee of the resurrection of the body. In commenting on Romans 8:24, "We are saved by hope," he writes, in what is certainly a 'stretching' of the text: "Already the flesh taken of us in the Lord is saved not in hope but in fact. For in our Head our flesh hath risen again and ascended whole."[129] In yet another of his disquisitions on Paul's "Flesh and blood shall not inherit the kingdom of God,"[130] Augustine writes: "As far as regards the substance, even then it shall be flesh. For even after the resurrection, the body of Christ was called flesh."[131]

It is very important to our understanding of Augustine's teaching on the resurrection of the body to notice that the resurrection is not, for him, a way to avoid facing death, a "defense against death."[132] In _De civitate Dei_ XIII.3, Augustine raises the question: "Is death, which separates soul and body, really a good thing for the good?"[133] Ambrose would have no difficulty with an affirmative answer.[134] But Augustine answers differently: ". . . the death of the body, the separation of the soul from the body, is not a good for anyone.[135] It is rather a "harsh and unnatural experience,"[136] since body and soul are joined by a "natural appetite" which hinders the soul in its quest for happiness until its body is returned to it."[137] In _Sermo_ CCXLI.4, Augustine uses the argument of the natural affinity of body and soul to refute the philosophers' explanation of reincarnation which is unconsciously based, he says, precisely on this affinity:

> After long ages, when [the soul's] former miseries have been completely forgotten, they experience a longing to return into bodies. . . . They return. Why? Because it gives them pleasure to live again in their bodies. How does this pleasure arise unless through the memory that they once dwelt in the body? . . . These philosophers say that, from love of their bodies, souls that are cleansed, purified, and wise will return to bodies.[138]

The reluctant admission of the soul's longing for its body, Augustine says, is in contradiction with the philosophers' claim that the disembodied soul is in its optimal state. He writes, in _De civitate Dei_ XIII.19:

> Although we must never for a moment doubt that the souls of the righteous and devout live in a state of rest after their departure from this life, yet they would be in a better state if they were living in conjunction with their bodies in perfect health.[139]

In a text which Augustine will come to use again and again as the paradigm of spontaneous love, he writes in _De doctrina christiana_ I.24.24:

> Neither does any man hate his own body. For the Apostle says truly, 'No man ever hated his own flesh' (Ephesians V.29).

> And when some say that they would rather be without a body altogether, they entirely deceive themselves. For it is not their body, but its heaviness and corruption that they hate. And so it is not no body, but an uncorrupted and very light body that they want.[140]

Augustine presents death as an evil; his descriptions of the resurrection never gloss over this painful inevitability. The point is rather that even death, the final enemy of mortal life, becomes an instrument of life.[141] The best that can be hoped for in the experience of physical death is that, patiently tolerated, it will augment the merit of patience.[142]

iii

There is no clear emphasis which distinguishes the mature Augustine's thought on resurrection of the body from that of his old age. Thus I have inevitably interwoven these periods in the foregoing discussion. However, two aspects of his last years may be remarked on: (1) the curious strengthening of dualism precisely at the time when his conscious assimilation and integration of the classical dualism of mind and body was most developed, and (2) his growing obsession with death.

1. It is outside the purview of this dissertation to discuss Augustine's views on predestination. Part of his attachment to the detailed exposition of this subject in his last years is explainable by the external pressure of the Pelagian controversy. But two aspects of the subjective part of Augustine's focus on predestination relate to our topic. First, by his late mature years, Augustine had managed the monumental task of integrating the body into his systematic intellectual picture of the meaning of human being; he had woven this conceptual scheme into the fabric of his consciousness so that it permeated and infused this consciousness. Nevertheless, as we have seen, there remain some unconscious and contradictory elements which conflict with his consciously integrated system of belief. And Augustine has transmuted his lingering psychological predilection for a dualistic structure of reality into predestinarianism; his dualism has gone underground in a conceptual scheme which interprets

the mysteries of human destiny in a manner which is admittedly dualistic but not incompatible with Christian faith. The dualism is no longer the external antagonism of body and soul, but a subtle subjective dualism which describes the divergence of human lives. The very thoroughness and skill with which Augustine has reoriented his conscious intellectual operation to integrate the body and reject the dualism of body and soul requires that lingering contradictory inclinations toward dualism--too rooted and temperamental to be consciously malleable--be repressed. Predestinarianism is the residue of dualism which Augustine failed to recognize and integrate consciously.

Conceptually, the doctrine of predestination expresses the experiential insight that "we are in the order of freedom, that is, in the order of that which is capable of not being,"[143] and that choices--the dozen choices a day between being and non-being which together constitute our life choice[144]--lie ultimately beyond our powers of conscious determination. Predestination formulates the fact of Augustine's experience and observation that some people receive precisely that which is needed at the time it is needed--grace; for other people there is simply no such availability of that which is needed at the time it is needed.

Secondly, the idea of grace is the fundamental αρχή of the old Augustine; the impenetrable experiential mystery of human freedom, which precedes even faith in God and from which this faith is derivative,[145] is intimately linked with the dualism of Augustine's old age. The "discovery of humility"[146] is the discovery that the source of human liberty is outside us.[147] In the intellectual sphere, the recognition of grace is the "modesty of thought"[148] which affirms the process of understanding as a process of aligning oneself with a transcendent source of truth which grants the next insight, not the final or absolute insight. In the moral and emotional sphere, grace describes the recognition that "the proper way to attain happiness is to be given it."[149]

The old Augustine is speaking from a vantage point in which the facts of his observation and experience of human beings had been sorted; the ambiguities of experience resolved themselves into categories that worked for Augustine. It is a result of the stage of life in which Augustine speaks, the result of a very adequate and workable intellectual synthesis in intimate conjunction with an increasing and pressing awareness of bodily limitations.[150]

2. Although Augustine remarks, in De vera religione and in the Confessions, that "it is the sinner, not the saint, who feels threatened by the transience of earthly things,"[151] by A.D. 417-418 when he wrote Book XIII of De civitate Dei, the theme of mortality "reappears like an obsession."[152]

> There is no one, it goes without saying, who is not nearer to death this year than he was last year, nearer tomorrow than today, today than yesterday, who will not by and by be nearer than he is at the moment, or is not nearer at the present time than he was a little while ago. Any space of time that we live through leaves us so much less time to live, and the remainder decreases with every passing day; so that the whole of our lifetime is nothing but a race towards death, in which no one is allowed the slightest pause or any slackening of the pace. All are driven on at the same speed and hurried along the same road to the same goal.[153]

Augustine does not repress his obsession with death, but uses it consciously--redeems it--to energize his belief and teaching on the resurrection of the body. Van Bavel has remarked on a perceptible difference in Augustine's teaching concerning the fear of death before and after A.D. 415.[154] Before 415 he considered fear of death to be suffered only by the weakest Christians and 'normally' overcome by the great majority; "in a great number of texts, he identified it simply with love of the earthly life."[155] But after that date, Augustine considered the fear of death to be 'natural'; even Peter and Paul suffered from it.[156] Yet the longing for God could dissipate the fear of death; however, it is only at the point at which the intensity of this longing becomes greater than the most primitive life urge, the instinct for survival, that one truly overcomes the fear of death.[157] The belief in the resurrection of the body is the necessary and sufficient catalyst for effecting this transformation of the life energy:

> I know you want to keep on living. You do not want to die. And you want to pass from this life to another in such a way that you will not rise again as a dead man, but fully alive and transformed. This is what you desire. This is the deepest human feeling: mysteriously, the soul itself wishes and instinctively desires it.[158]

In conclusion, Augustine's mature expositions of the resurrection of the body make use of two major arguments; the bodily resurrection is--to a great degree--experiential in that its perfect metaphor is the human body and human experience, and it is nonexperiential in that the transience and corruptibility of the mortal body makes it difficult to imagine a state in which these elements will be eliminated, but it is modeled in the resurrection body of Christ. Augustine saw that the belief in the resurrection of the body acknowledges and integrates the unending affinity of body and soul, and this awareness has permeated his consciousness to the extent that even his image of the relationship of body and soul has changed. In the early dialogues, Augustine uses the popular image of the body as servant of the soul; in _De civitate Dei_ XV.7.2, his image of the relationship is that of the body as 'spouse' of the soul, an image which he uses also to describe the intimate relationship of love between Christ and the Church.[159]

All of Augustine's descriptions of the resurrection demonstrate his concern to find images which render this central dogma of Christian faith concrete and living to people. Augustine recognized that one does not want resurrection of the body if the body is not gratifying now; that is why the whole focus of Book XXII of _De civitate Dei_ is on the intrinsic pleasure of bodily existence. It is the apex of his argument for resurrection of the body. The movement of his discussion is from the external, sensible evidence of miracles (XXII.3 through XXII.10), to meeting objections and difficulties of pagans and Christians with the bodily resurrection, to a catalogue of the miseries, anxieties, and dangers of the mortal body--all in setting the context--as a brilliant and skillful rhetorical building toward what he considers his ultimate argument, the unimpeachable goodness and beauty of the human body. And the first example of this goodness which Augustine lists is the function of reproduction, "inherent and interwoven in human bodies,"[160] the "miraculous combination of an immaterial with a material substance."[161] The next evidence of goodness of human being which Augustine presents is the power of the mind; finally, the body itself is presented as evidence of "the goodness of God and the providence of the mighty Creator," specifically and in detail, the beauty and gratification of the body. All that is necessary for unending happiness is the falling away of the accretions of corruption and concupiscence. The body, delivered, not from sexuality but from the compulsive hegemony of unintegrated sexuality, and from the anxiety of death, will be the perfect condition of blessedness. The final chapter of Augustine's great epic, De civitate Dei, images the life of the resurrection body:

> All the limbs and organs of the body, no longer subject to decay, the parts which we now see assigned to various essential functions, will then be freed from all such constraint, since full, secure, certain and eternal felicity will have displaced necessity; and all those parts will contribute to the praise of God. For even those elements in the bodily harmony of which I have already spoken, the harmonies which, in our present state, are hidden, will then be hidden no longer. Dispersed internally and externally, throughout the whole body, and combined with other great and marvelous things that will then be revealed, they will kindle our rational minds to the praise of the great Artist by the delight afforded by a beauty that satisfies the reason.[162]

What Augustine images here is no longer the abstract intellectual pleasure of a mind, not only distinguished, but isolated from the body, but the happiness of the whole human being, based on the bodily experience--the coenesthesis--of perfect presence. He has built carefully to this conclusion, fully aware of its difficulty for both 'the philosophers' and ordinary people, pagans and Christians.[163]

> And the whole Gospel given through Christ is this, brethren, and nothing else: the resurrection--resurrection not only of soul but of body. Both were dead, the body from infirmity, the soul from iniquity. . . . The soul can rise again only in virtue of Christ's Godhead: the body only in virtue of his manhood.[164]

CHAPTER VI

CONCLUSION

We have investigated Augustine's conscious integration of the meaning and value of the body; we have also seen that there are areas of ambivalence in which this integration is not complete. Our task in the conclusion of this dissertation will be (1) to interpret the data of this study in a way which illuminates Augustine's accomplishment in a historical and psychological perspective, however tentative and evocative, and (2) to indicate some possible reasons for the nearly universal contemporary consensus that it is Augustine that was the originator, in Western thought, of denigration of the body.

In the eyes of classical philosophers, the integration of the body was, as Rutilius Namatianus put it, a "fleeing from the light," a radical departure from the 'light' of classical antiquity which was characterized by the differentiation and hegemony of the mind. For Christian thinkers, the body became the condition of learning, trial, and victory, the intimate companion of the soul in pain and joy.[1] In the metaphor of the alchemical task of differentiation and reunification described in the Introduction (p. 3), Jung identifies the Christian standpoint with the _unio mentalis_, the overcoming of the body.[2] If Jung's views were correct, the Christian task would be simply a continuation of the philosophical task which reached its full articulation in Aristotle. Rather, the task of Christian thinkers--and their historical and psychological significance--lay in reuniting the _unio mentalis_ with the body.

The Church fathers instinctively realized that the Incarnation 'settles' the question of the value of the body; yet it remained difficult to describe precisely _how_. They looked to philosophy for help in understanding it; even those among them who claimed to disdain philosophy--Tertullian and Ambrose, for example--set their description of the meaning and value of the body in the framework of a philosophical system; even more subtly and pervasively, they accepted as normative the model of human being as a 'mixture,' and the problem as that of describing the relationship of higher and lower parts.

It was Augustine who first brought to conscious realization and painstaking systematic articulation the task of reuniting soul and body, that is, of uniting consistent intellectual formulation with the deepest human longing.[3] It was he who, not content to "affirm without a shred of understanding," worked out the implications of the soul's love for its body, and sought more adequate metaphors to express it. Augustine formulated no new Christian dogmas; he worked within a well-defined tradition, but his emphases and the images he presented demonstrate his sensitivity both to the universe of discourse within which he worked and the repressed longing of human beings for wholeness: "I wish the whole to be healthy, since I am the whole."[4] We have seen him move, in the decade following his conversion, from preoccupation with overcoming the body to--especially in the last fifteen years of his life--a growing obsession with resurrection of the body: "Perfect health of body shall be the ultimate immortality of the whole man."[5] His historical importance lies in the fact that he influenced not only his own age but the whole Western tradition.

Ironically, the name of Augustine is vehemently associated in our time--which prides itself on increasing preoccupation with the body--with sexual repression and denigration of the body. We can suggest several reasons for this association, some cultural and some personal to Augustine. As Freud has said, the first conscious response to the irruption into consciousness of repressed or denied longings is emphatic denial;[6] an increment of conscious integration always escalates unconscious resistance. There is more than a perceptible element of emphatic denial of the Christian integration of the body in those aspects of fourth-century asceticism which demonstrate the belligerent contempt and "systematic warfare"[7] against the body which is expressed in the statement of one of the desert fathers: "I am killing it because it is killing me."[8] This kind of rejection and hatred of the body, which sometimes went much further in Christians than in pagans,[9] inevitably accompanied the rapid popularization of Christian ideas in the fourth century. The growth of Christianity is inextricably mingled with the vehement denial of precisely that element which was being most strongly integrated on the conscious level.

"The quality of a religious system depends perhaps less on its specific doctrine than on the choice of problems that it regards as important."[10] This, I think, gets to the heart of the question. Augustine sharpened the focus--and the anxiety--by bringing to consciousness the task of integrating the body. We have seen Augustine in the process--never completed in his lifetime--of moving from thought and behavior that assumed that Christianity ultimately required sacrifice of embodiment to thought and activity that integrated the body. Two centuries before, Tertullian had thought in terms of a different kind of sacrifice, sacrificium intellectus. A century and a half before, Origen had presumably thought that the sacrifice of his sexuality was required. Augustine found no real difficulty with integrating intellect, but he pointed to sexuality as the one 'great force'[11] which eluded stable integration. There is still a flavor of the early Augustine's philosophical orientation in his complaint that sexual desire clashes "inevitably and permanently with reason,"[12] but the stronger frustration was the overwhelming difficulty of integrating it with the will,[13] the vehicle of holistic expression of the human person. For himself, he found the best possibility to be the celibate sublimation we have described. As a Christian teacher, he worked hard to overcome his personal predilection. Yet his choice of problems focused on the body. And there is still, in Augustine, a strong unconscious tendency to sacrifice what he despairs of integrating; he is not fully resigned to a daily process of slow, and perhaps unsteady, growth.[14] One suspects that the more conscious intellectual work he did on revaluing the body, the more unconscious resistance he experienced, so that--predictably--the period of greatest conscious affirmation of the body--Augustine's old age--coincides exactly with the time of his strongest negative focus on sexuality. There is, in Augustine, an element of unconscious emphatic denial of exactly that which is consciously affirmed. In this sense, the popular association of repression of the body with Augustine is accurate.

But there is also a real area of misunderstanding. From a little reading of Augustine, one can easily select passages which apparently substantiate the view that it is Augustine we have to blame for centuries of repression and contempt for the body:

> Recognize in thyself something within, within thyself. Leave thou abroad both they clothing and thy flesh; descend into thyself; go to thy secret chamber, thy mind. . . . For not in the body but in the mind was man made in the image of God.[15]

> Let [the mind], if it can, raise itself for a little above the body and above those things which it is wont to perceive through the bodily senses and let it contemplate what that is which uses the body as its instrument.[16]

> . . . by degrees I passed from bodies to the soul.[17]

What we have in these passages are not pejorative evaluations of the body, but specific mystical instruction, parallels for which can be found in the mystical writings of both East and West.[18] Augustine's two accounts of mystical experiences[19] both describe this method of gradual withdrawal of energy and attention from external objects to the immutable being which informs them. But it is only one alternative method for penetrating more deeply into the invisible which Augustine presents; the method which he expounds far more frequently is that of penetrating more deeply into the visible:

> But what do I love when I love you? Not the beauty of the body nor the glory of time, not the brightness of light shining so friendly to the eye, not the sweet and various melodies of singing, not the fragrance of flowers and unguents and spices, not manna and honey, not limbs welcome to the embraces of the flesh: it is not these that I love when I love my God. And yet I do love a kind of light, melody, fragrance, food, embracement when I love my God; for he is the light, the melody, the fragrance, the food, the embracement of my inner being where there is a brilliance that space cannot contain, a sound that time cannot carry away, a perfume that no breeze disperses, a taste undiminished by eating, a clinging together that no satiety will sunder. This is what I love when I love my God.[20]

It is only the distressing mutability of sensible objects and of the body itself--which senses and enjoys these objects--that disturbs Augustine: "Take away death, the last enemy, and my own flesh shall be my dear friend throughout eternity."[21] There is no pejorative esteem of the body on the basis of its lack of value in the mature Augustine.

Nowhere in the late classical philosophical attempts to describe the relationship of soul and body do we find the body unambiguously scorned and disparaged. Among both pagans and Christians the clearest thinkers agreed that the body was not of itself evil, that a metaphysical dualism was an inadequate foundation for thought. Yet an irreducible existential dualism remained, and less rigorous thinkers opted for a cosmology and anthropology which explained and supported it.[22] The young Augustine felt the attraction of such a system; the old Augustine still felt the attraction poignantly, but he also realized the inadequacy of resolving an experiential tension by metaphysical descriptions which destroy the unity of human being. Despite his own unconscious resistance and that of his culture to the revaluing of the body, Augustine has done a herculean task of integrating the "stone which the builders rejected." The body became the cornerstone of his theology.

CHAPTER I

NOTES

[1]Sigmund Freud, Collected Papers, ed. J. Riviere and J. Strachey (New York: International Psychoanalytical Press, 1924-50), V, 181-182; C. N. Cochrane has described the intellectual aspect of this process in Christianity and Classical Culture (London: Oxford University Press, 1940), chap. 11, pp. 399-455.

[2]Hegel's term, from the Preface to The Phenomenology of Mind.

[3]Aristotle, Nichomachean Ethics, trans. J. A. K. Thomson (Baltimore: Penguin Books, 1953), esp. Bk. I.7.

[4]Simone Pétrement, Le Dualisme chez Platon, Les Gnostiques et Les Manichéens (Paris: Presses Universitaires de France, 1947), p. 32.

[5]Ibid., p. 8.

[6]H.-I. Marrou, "La résurrection des morts et las apologistes des premiers siècles," Lumière et Vie 3 (April 1952); 86: The Stoics' "morale n'est pas moins rigoureuse à l'égard du corps que celle des dualistes les plus sévères."

[7]"Le dualisme non métaphysique est le dualisme original. Le dualisme métaphysique est artificiel et tombe dans toutes sortes de difficultés." Pétrement, p. 301.

[8]Carl Jung, Mysterium Coniunctionis (New York: Bollingen Series XX, 1963), p. 418.

[9]Ibid., p. 474.

[10]Paraphrased by Ernest Evans, Tertullian's Treatise on the Incarnation (London: S.P.C.K., 1956), p. xxi.

[11]J. A. T. Robinson has demonstrated the Pauline use of σῶμα and σάρξ to be an extension of the Hebrew usage in which they are used, not as parts of man but as "the whole person considered from different points of view," that is, as synecdoche. "While σάρξ stands for man in the solidarily of creation in his distance from God, σῶμα stands for man, in the solidarity of creation, as made for God." The Body: A Study in Pauline Theology (London: SCM Press, 1952), p. 31.

[12]A.-M. Bonnardière, "La date du 'De concupiscentia' de S. Augustin," Revue des Etudes Augustiniennes 1 (1959): 122.

[13]The bibliography is extensive; I follow R. J. O'Connell's listing of the works of Plotinus with which Augustine was familiar in St. Augustine's Early Theory of Man (Cambridge, Mass.:

Harvard University Press, 1968), somewhat modified by John J. O'Meara's discussion of Porphyry's influence in Porphyry's Philosophy from Oracles in Augustine (Paris: Etudes Augustiniennes, 1959).

[14] M. Ward, ed., France Pagan? (New York: Sheed & Ward, 1949), p. 77.

[15] Pétrement, p. 34.

[16] Jean Guitton, The Modernity of St. Augustine (Baltimore: Helicon Press, 1959), p. 79.

[17] Solil. I.xiv.24. Translation: Erich Przywara, An Augustine Synthesis (New York: Harper & Row, 1958), p. 1.

[18] Dated by Peter Brown at A.D. 416-17; Augustine of Hippo (Berkeley: University of California Press, 1969), p. 282.

[19] E. Gilson, Introduction à l'Etude de saint Augustin, 2nd ed. (Paris, 1943), p. 58.

CHAPTER II

NOTES

[1]Sister Mary Ann Ida Gannon, "The Active Theory of Sensation in St. Augustine," The New Scholasticism 30 (1956): 154-180.

[2]Peter Brown, "Society and the Supernatural" (unpublished lectures presented at University of California, January 1975).

[3]De quant. anim. 23.41.

[4]R. Nash, The Light of the Mind (Lexington: University of Kentucky Press, 1969), p. 43.

[5]G. H. Clark, "Plotinus' Theory of Sensation," Philosophical Review 51 (1942): 358.

[6]Stoicorum Veterum Fragmenta ii.83; hereafter referred to as SVF.

[7]A. A. Long, Hellenistic Philosophy (New York: Charles Scribner's Sons, 1974), p. 124.

[8]Ibid., p. 126.

[9]Enn. IV.2.1; trans. Stephen MacKenna, Plotinus: The Enneads, 2nd ed. (New York: Pantheon Books, 1956). This translation is used for the Enneads IV-VI unless otherwise indicated.

[10]Enn. IV.3.26.

[11]'Matter' and 'body,' it is well to note, are by no means identical in Plotinus, nor, for that matter, in the Stoics; matter, the principle of evil, of resistance, of limit, communicates its own weakness to the bodies based on it. "The difference between matter and a body is that the latter is animated while the former is not." R. E. Buckenmeyer, "St. Augustine and the Life of Man's Body in the Early Dialogues," Augustinian Studies 3 (1962): 142; see also De ord. II.6.19; Contra acad. III.17.38.

[12]Enn. V.1.6; Enn. III.4.3.

[13]Enn. III.6.

[14]Gannon, p. 177, n. 82.

[15]R. A. Markus, Marius Victorinus and Augustine," Cambridge History of Later Greek and Early Medieval Philosophy, ed. A. H. Armstrong (Cambridge: University Press, 1970); hereafter referred to as CHLGEMP.

[16]R. T. Wallis, _Neoplatonism_ (New York: Charles Scribner's Sons, 1972), p. 111; see also _Enn_. I.1.4; IV.3.22.

[17]_Enn_. IV.3.26; see also _Enn_. I.1.7; IV.4.14; VI.4.15.

[18]R. P. Thonnard, "Notes Complementaires" on Bk. VI, _De musica_ (Paris: Bibliothèque Augustinienne) 7:518; see also _Enn_. III.6.2.

[19]_Enn_. V.5.7.

[20]_Solil_. I.14.24; _Contra acad_. II.1.2; III.11.16.

[21]E. L. Fortin, _Christianisme et Culture Philosophique au Cinquième Siècle_ (Paris: Etudes Augustiniennes, 1959), pp.133-134.

[22]Ibid., p. 9.

[23]Clement, _Stromata_ V.8.42.2; VII.5.28.1; Origen, _Contra Celsum_ VI.71; _De oratione_ 23.1; _De principiis_ II.1.3.

[24]_CHLGEMP_, p. 360.

[25]_De quant. anim_ 23.41: "Sensum puto esse, non latere animam quod patitur corpus." "The expression _non latet_ is based on the μη λαδειν of Plotinus." Gilson, _The Christian Philosophy of St. Augustine_ (New York: Random House, 1960), p. 277; hereafter referred to as _Christian Philosophy_. See _Enn_. IV.4.19.

[26]Gareth Matthews, "The Inner Man," in _Augustine: A Collection of Critical Essays_, R. A. Markus ed. (New York: Doubleday, 1972), pp. 87-88.

[27]Nash, p. 41.

[28]Gilson, _Christian Philosophy_, p. 61.

[29]Ibid., p. 63; see also _De mus_. VI.5.12.

[30]_De mus_. VI.8.21.

[31]_De mus_. VI.4: "mirare potius quod facere aliquid in anima corpus potest."

[32]Nash, p. 45; see _De quant. anim_. 33.71; _De mus_. VI.5.9-10.

[33]Nash, p. 46; but there may be another, more precise reason for Augustine's departure from Neoplatonic theory here--the strong Stoic influence described below.

[34]Ibid., p. 48.

[35]_De quant. anim_. 23.43.

[36]J. Rohmer, "L'intentionalité des sensations chez saint Augustine," _Augustinus Magister_ 1 (1954): 493-494.

[37]Ibid., p. 494; Rohmer suggests that the statement of *De musica* VI: "ego enim ab anima hoc corpus animari non puto nisi intentione facientis," should be translated: "J'estime qui l'âme anime le corps par l'intentionnalité de ses actes.' Ceci posé, tout le passage s'explique. L'âme ne subit rien de la part du corps, mais agit en lui."

[38]R. J. O'Connell, "*De libero arbitrio*: Stoicism Revisited," *Augustinian Studies* 1 (1970): 54. See also Charles Baguette, "Une period stoicienne dans l'évolution de la pensée de s. Augustin," *Revue des Etudes Augustiniennes* 16 (1970): 47-77, for evidence of Stoicism's attractiveness to Augustine.

[39]O'Connell, p. 50.

[40]Michael Spanneut, *Le Stoicisme des Pères de l'Église* (Paris: University of Paris Press, 1957), p. 396.

[41]Ibid., p. 430.

[42]*De mus*. VI.5.8: "Quo quid miserius, quid detestabilius credi potest?"

[43]Ibid.

[44]Buckenmeyer, pp. 133-134.

[45]Nash, p. 41; see also Robert Ornstein, *The Psychology of Consciousness* (San Francisco: W. H. Freeman, 1972), p. 216: "The primary job of the brain is to control the body."

[46]*De quant. anim*. 28.55.

[47]Buckenmeyer, p. 138.

[48]*De ord*. I.2.3.

[49]*De ord*. II.18.47; see also Buckenmeyer, p. 146.

[50]Ship and harbor: *Solil*. I.4.9; *De ord*. II.19.51; *Contra acad*. III.2.2-3; the meaning of a word (*significatio*) as analogous to soul, its sound (*sonus*) to body: *De quant. anim*. 32.67, etc.

[51]*Enn*. IV.4.24.

[52]*Enn*. IV.4.22.

[53]*Enn*. IV.3.29.

[54]*Enn*. I.1.19.

[55]*Enn*. V.3.1.

[56]Gordon Clark, "Plotinus' Theory of Sensation," *The Philosophical Review* 51 (1942): 379.

[57]*Enn*. IV.8.7.

[58]"Perfecta autem anima aversatur materiam . . . divinis intendit, terrenem autem materiam fugit." De Isaac et Anima III.6.

[59]Expositio in Lucam I.31; I.6; De Abraham II.4.13; II.8.46.

[60]Clark, p. 381.

[61]As Gilson has remarked in another context, "The way to keep anything from being lost is to put everything in its proper place." Christian Philosophy, p. 121. It is in this spirit that Plotinus puts sensation "in its place."

[62]Enn. IV.8.8.

[63]Enn. IV.4.23.

[64]Clark, p. 382.

[65]De mus. VI.4.7.

[66]This analogy was apparently taken from Plato's Theaetetus.

[67]De mus. VI.5.8.

[68]V. Bourke, Augustine's Quest of Wisdom (Milwaukee: Bruce Publishing Co., 1945), p. 202 and p. 304.

[69]Retract. II.24.1.

[70]De gen. ad litt. XII.24.51.

[71]Ibid., VII.28.

[72]Gilson, Christian Philosophy, p. 58.

[73]Clark, p. 375.

[74]Gannon, p. 172; see also Ep. VII; Solil. II.20.35.

[75]Clark, p. 375.

[76]De gen. ad litt. XII.8.19: "ubi sunt significationes velut imagines rerum ac similitudines, . . ."

[77]P. Agaisse et A. Solignac, "Notes," in Ouevres de Saint Augustin, Series VII, vol. 49, De Genesi ad litteram (Paris: Desclée de Brouwer, 1974), p. 562.

[78]De gen. ad litt. XII.11.22.

[79]Ibid., XII.24.51.

[80]W. A. Schumacher, Spiritus and Spiritualis: A Study in the Sermons of St. Augustine (Mundelein, Ill.: St. Mary of the Lake Seminary Press, 1957), pp. 23-24.

[81]Ibid.

[82]Ibid., p. 23.

[83]G. Verbeke, *L'évolution de la doctrine du pneuma du Stoicisme à S. Augustin* (Paris: Desclée de Brouwer, 1945), pp. 364-366.

[84]Schumacher, p. 23.

[85]Cf. Bonsirven, *L'Evangile de Paul* (Aubier: Editions Montaigne, 1948), pp. 104-105.

[86]Schumacher, p. 120.

[87]Ibid.

[88]Ibid., p. 24; *Serm*. CXXVIII.9, dated between A.D. 412 and 416; *De anim. et ejus orig*., dated A.D. 420-421.

[89]Solignac, p. 565. But Verbeke's discussion of the important differences between Porphyry's pneumatology and Augustine's *spiritus* as a power of the soul must not be overlooked. Porphyry's πνεῦμα is a psychic envelope: "le *spiritus* d'Augustin, tout en étant subordonné à l'intelligence, fait cependant partie de l'âme immatérielle, tandis que le caractère matériel de l'enveloppe pneumatique des néoplatoniciens est incontestable" (p. 504).

[90]Schumacher, p. 120.

[91]*De gen. ad litt*. XII.7.16.

[92]Gannon, p. 163; see also *De gen. ad litt*. XII.11.22.

[93]Rohmer, pp. 492-493.

[94]"Il la chargera d'opérer la soudure entre le processus organique et sa détermination venue de l'objet extérieur et de rendre celui-ci présent a l'âme elle-même. L'*intentio* résume donc la sensation dans sons processus intérieur perçu par la conscience. Nous avons là une traduction spiritualiste à la fois de la συνέντασις et de la κατάληψισ que les Stoiciens attribuaient à l'ésprit vital pour expliquer la προαβολῆ, la projection des qualités sensibles sur l'objet senti. En attribuant à l'âme seule la faculté d'intentionner les fonctions organiques, il a simplifié et clarifié la théorie stoicienne sur un point capital de notre connaissance." Ibid., p. 493.

[95]Nash, p. 40; see also *De Civitate Dei* VII.7.

[96]*De Trin*. XI.9.16.

[97]*De Trin*. XI.2.3.

[98]Verbeke, p. 505.

[99]A. N. M. Rich, "Body and Soul in the Philosophy of

Plotinus," Journal of the History of Philosophy 1 (1963): 3.

[100]De gen. ad litt. XII.24.51.

[101]Verbeke, p. 503.

[102]Gannon, p. 170.

[103]Cf. Enn. IV.5.4; discussing whether the visual ray is necessary because there is a body in the interval between the eye and the object, or because there is an interval, Plotinus writes: ". . . if it is because of the interval simply, one would need to assume that the visual object is inert and completely inactive. But this is impossible."

[104]The description of sensation was highly important to Plotinus: Clark, p. 357, points out that "in every Ennead except the second, the primary subjects of the tractates force his consideration of sensation and of the relation of the sensible world to the world above."

[105]Clark, p. 359.

[106]Ibid., p. 364.

[107]Ibid., p. 359.

[108]Enn. V.3.1; V.3.2-3.

[109]Enn V.42.

[110]De Trin. VIII.6.9.

[111]Frederick Copleston, A History of Philosophy, II (Westminster, Md.: Newman Press, 1946), 60.

[112]De Trin. IX.11.6.

[113]Trans. Pryzwara, p. 9.

[114]Gannon, p. 170; see also De Trin. XV.12.21.

[115]An interesting parallel development of emphasis from metaphysical speculation to moral admonition occurred in Plotinus: "when he was young and mature he wrote mostly of the beauty of the spiritual world and ecstasy . . . when he was old he wrote almost exclusively on moral subjects." Pierre Hadot, Plotin ou la Simplicité du Regard (Paris: Librarie Plon, 1963), p. 91.

[116]Gilson, The Christian Philosophy of St. Thomas Aquinas, trans. L. K. Shook (New York: Random House, 1956), p. 149.

[117]R. A. Markus, "Alienatio: Philosophy and Eschatology in the Development of an Augustinian Idea," Studia Patristica 9 (1966): 431-450.

[118]Gaston Bachelard, The Poetics of Space (New York: Orion Press, 1964), p. xii.

[119]De gen. ad litt. XII.16.33.

[120]Gannon, p. 171; see Markus, Saeculum: History and Society in the Theology of St. Augustine (Cambridge: Cambridge University Press, 1970), p. 11: "Few Christian theologians can equal the inwardness of Augustine's sense of the mutabilitas rerum humanarum and the poetic imagery in which it finds expression in his work."

[121]Markus, p. 79.

[122]Augustine regarded the study of Scripture, its understanding and exposition, to be the very center of the bishop's activities; Conf. XI.2.2.

[123]In Ps. CXXI.6.

[124]This occurs as early as the Cassiciacum dialogues and increases in frequency and richness in his mature writings; see also Solil. I.14.24.

[125]Trans. Przywara, p. 8.

[126]So that, for example, bodily things cannot affect the soul in any way.

[127]Conf. X.40.

[128]Peter Brown, Augustine of Hippo, p. 151.

[129]Schumacher, p. 118.

[130]De lib. arb. II.16.41; as P. Brown writes, "Augustine himself always resented traveling: he always associated it with a sense of protracted labor and of the infinite postponement of his dearest wishes." Augustine of Hippo, p. 153.

[131]De vera relig. XXV.47.

[132]De vera relig., dated 390. Brown, Augustine of Hippo, p. 415.

[133]Brown, Augustine of Hippo, pp. 416-417.

[134]Retract. I.12.7; I.13.5.

[135]F. Van der Meer, Augustine the Bishop, trans. Brian Battershaw and G. R. Lamb (London: Sheed & Ward, 1961), p. 540.

[136]Brown, Augustine of Hippo, p. 414.

[137]Ibid., p. 378.

[138]This may be the basis for the assertion of A. H. M. Jones, The Later Roman Empire, II (Oxford: Blackwell, 1964), 963-964, that Augustine's later acceptance of and emphasis on miracles was a sudden and unprepared collapse into popular credulity.

[139]Gilson, Christian Philosophy, pp. 33-34.

[140]Augustine: City of God, trans. Henry Bettenson (Baltimore: Penguin Books, 1972), p. 1034. De civ. Dei XXII.8.1.

[141]De civ. Dei XXII.9.

[142]Only the resurrection of Christ in the flesh could "result in the power to work such marvels." De civ. Dei XXII.9.

[143]Ibid., XXII.8.

[144]In Joan. Evang. VIII.1. Trans.: Homilies on the Gospel According to St. John, 2 vols. (Oxford University Press, 1848-49), vol. 1.

[145]Brown, Augustine of Hippo, p. 416.

[146]De Trin. III.2.6. Trans. Przywara, p. 44.

[147]In Joan. Evang. VIII.I.

[148]Rainer Maria Rilke nicely captures Augustine's understanding of the miracle of the natural: "We had a different conception of the marvelous, we found that if everything happened naturally that would always be the most marvelous." The Notebooks of Malte Laurids Brigge (New York: W. W. Norton, 1949), p. 88.

[149]Brown, Augustine of Hippo, p. 417; De civ. Dei XXII.90.

[150]De civ. Dei XXII.22.

[151]See n. 142, above.

[152]Serm. CCLXXVII.5-6.

CHAPTER III

NOTES

[1]James Hillman, "The Language of Psychology and the Speech of the Soul," Eranos Jahrbuch: The Mystic Vision (New York: Pantheon Books, 1966), p. 315.

[2]Sermones in Cantica Canticorum 61.8; trans. E. Auerbach, Literary Language and Its Public in Late Latin Antiquity and in the Middle Ages (London: Kegal Paul, 1965), pp. 70-71.

[3]Bernard O'Kelly, The Renaissance Image of Man and the World (Columbus: Ohio State University Press, 1966), p. 9.

[4]De perfectione vitae ad sorores VI.

[5]E. Auerbach, Mimesis: The Representation of Reality in Western Literature (Princeton: Princeton University Press, 1953), pp. 71-72.

[6]Peter Brown, "Society and the Supernatural" (unpublished lectures presented at the University of California, Berkeley, Winter 1975).

[7]Tertullian, De Anima 55.

[8]W. H. Frend, Martyrdom and Persecution in the Early Church (Oxford: Basil Blackwell, 1965), p. 356.

[9]Brown, unpublished lectures.

[10]Ambrose, De virginitate I.2; I.5.

[11]Barlaam and Joasaph, ed. Woodward and Mattingly (London: W. Heinemann, 1914); see also Vit. Ant. 47: "daily martyr to his conscience, ever fighting the battles of the faith."

[12]Frend, p. 548.

[13]Quoted by Frend, p. 555.

[14]Frend, p. 547; Eusebius, Historia ecclesiastica VII.32.30.

[15]Jung also posits such a system: Über psychische Energetik und das Wesen der Traume (Zurich: Rascher, 1948).

[16]See Patanjali's description of the purpose of Yoga: "Yoga consists in the intentional stopping of the spontaneous activity of the mind stuff," and J. Campbell's discussion of this: "The idea is that within the gross gray matter of the brain there is an active 'subtle substance' (sukshma) that is continually changing form. Responsive to sound, touch, sight, taste, smell, this

fluent inmost substance of the nerves takes on the shapes of all their sense impressions--which, indeed, is how and why we experience them. There is a difficulty, however, in that its movement never ceases. Any person unused to meditation, desiring to fix in his mind a single image or thought, will find within seconds that he is already entertaining associated thoughts. The untrained mind will not stand still, and Yoga is the intentional stopping of its movement." The Mythic Image (Princeton: Princeton University Press, 1974), p. 313; see De Trin. X.5.7: "Dat enim (anima) eis (corporum imaginibus) formandis quiddam substantiae suae."

[17] J. Custance, Wisdom, Madness and Folly (New York: Pellegrini & Cudahy, 1952), p. 171.

[18] E. R. Dodds, Pagan and Christian in an Age of Anxiety (New York: W. W. Norton, 1965), p. 29.

[19] Ibid.; Vita S. Antonii 45.909A.

[20] Cf. Regula Pachomii 30; Jerome, Ep. 107.11.

[21] Dodds, p. 30; for discussion of the original union of ψυχή, σῶμα, and their split in Greek thought, see Dodds, The Greeks and the Irrational (Berkeley: University of California Press, 1951), pp. 138 ff.

[22] Dodds, Pagan and Christian, p. 30.

[23] R. J. O'Connell, St. Augustine's Early Theory of Man 386-391, p. 184; hereafter referred to as Early Theory.

[24] "Any activity not transmitted to the sensitive faculty has not traversed the entire Soul: we remain unaware because the human being includes sense perception; man is not merely a part (the higher part) of the Soul, but the total." Ennead V.1.2.

[25] De mor. Eccl. cath. I.5.7.

[26] Plotinus, in his one polemical treatise, Against the Gnostics (II.9), affirms the significance of bodily acts.

[27] SVF ii.525.

[28] Long, p. 154.

[29] Ibid., p. 110.

[30] Ibid.; see also SVF i.178.202.

[31] J. M. Rist, Stoic Philosophy (Cambridge University Press, 1969), p. 52.

[32] Ibid., p. 130.

[33] A. H. Armstrong, Note 2 on Ennead I.4.13, Plotinus, 6 vols. (Harvard University Press; Loeb Classical Library, 1966), I, 204.

[34]Michel Spanneut, Le Stoicisme des Pères de l'Église (Paris: University of Paris Press, 1957), p. 430.

[35]Charles Baguette, "Une period stoicienne dans l'évolution de la pensée de S. Augustin," Revue des Etudes Augustiniennes 16 (1970): 47-77.

[36]M. Testard, S. Augustin et Ciceron, I (Paris: Etudes Augustiniennes, 1958), p. 142; see also Conf. VI.26.19.

[37]Iamblichus, De Anima 380.14-19; cf. Wallis, p. 35.

[38]Ibid.

[39]Ibid., p. 79.

[40]Pétrement, p. 338.

[41]A. H. Armstrong, "Neoplatonic Valuations of Nature, Body, and Intellect," Augustinian Studies 3 (1972): 42.

[42]Vita Plotini I.1-2.

[43]Enn. II.9.5.1-16.

[44]Enn. II.9.16.5-14.

[45]Wallis, p. 9.

[46]Enn. I.4.7.1-8.

[47]Enn. I.4.9-11, 14.

[48]"Ce n'est pas le corps qu'il combat mais un excès de vitalité physique qui risquerait de déséquilibrer l'âme." Hadot, p. 115.

[49]Enn. I.4.15.

[50]Enn. I.4.4.25-30.

[51]Enn. I.4.6.

[52]Wallis, p. 84; see also Enn. I.4.16; II.9.18.

[53]Enn. I.4.13; A. H. Armstrong, trans., Plotinus, p. 205. This translation is used for Enneads I-III unless otherwise stated.

[54]Enn. I.4.15; 'consider': βλέπη; to turn towards.

[55]Which Plotinus has just described as identification with the higher soul.

[56]O'Connell, Early Theory, p. 190.

[57]Brown, Augustine of Hippo, p. 68.

[58]O'Connell, Early Theory, p. 190.

[59]Piaget, in The Construction of Reality in the Child, has discussed the process by which a child formulates an operational relationship between self and world, and only then, when such functions as cause and effect, space, and time are manageable, does the child begin a specifically intellectual development. I conjecture that only when a certain stage of intellectual development has been attained is it possible for a person to begin a specifically religious development. Only when one has arrived at an intellectual impasse generated by the frustration of comprehending that the dualistic explanation, although it formulates experience, does not work when abstracted into a cosmology, can a properly religious development, that of relating the center of the self to the Center of the universe, take place; the religious question is one of relationship, not primarily of knowledge. Augustine's Manichaean period is one of intellectual, not religious, development. His fascination with Manichaeaism came from the motivations pointed to by Frend when he writes: "Manichaeism was the religion of those with inquiring minds and of ascetics." The Gnostic-Manichaean Tradition in Roman North Africa," Journal of Ecclesiastical History 4 (January-April 1953): 23.

[60]Conf. V.6.

[61]H.-C. Puech, "The Concept of Redemption in Manichaeism," The Mystic Vision, ed. J. Campbell (Princeton University Press, Bollingen Series XXX.6, 1968), p. 253.

[62]"illis manichaeorum longis fabulis." Conf. V.3.

[63]Puech, p. 250.

[64]This affinity for dualism is attested by the persistence of Manichaeism in North Africa from probably A.D. 277 to the first half of the eighth century through consistent persecution. Frend, "Gnostic-Manichaean Tradition," pp. 16-17.

[65]Dated by Brown at A.D. 392 (Augustine of Hippo, p. 74).

[66]John J. O'Meara, The Young Augustine (London: Longmans, Green, 1954), p. 159: ". . . the Manichaeans preached in season and out an exaggerated observance of bodily chastity. Their whole doctrine as it revealed itself in practice concentrated on this one point: the evil of reproduction and everything connected therewith. . . . It was not that Christianity was content with less in this matter, but rather that it made less of a fetish of it."

[67]C. C. Martindale, "A Sketch of the Life and Character of St. Augustine," St. Augustine: His Life and Thought (1930), p. 89: Authors write of the trivialities of Augustine's youthful sins "because they are not Africans or even Latins. I doubt if they know very well even their own world."

[68]O'Meara, The Young Augustine, p. 142.

[69]M. Testard, p. 26.

[70]Ibid., p. 145.

[71]Conf. VIII.2.27.

[72]Testard, p. 147.

[73]Conf. X.31.

[74]Dated by Brown at A.D. 388 (Augustine of Hippo, p. 74).

[75]De mor. eccl. cath. I.5.

[76]Ibid., I.27.

[77]Ibid., I.33.

[78]De mor. eccl. cath. I.33.

[79]De vera relig. XX.40.

[80]J. A. T. Robinson, The Body: A Study in Pauline Theology (London: SCM Press, 1952), p. 52.

[81]Ibid., p. 13.

[82]J. A. Beckaert, "Bases Philosophiques de l'acèse augustinienne," Augustinus Magister II (Etudes Augustiniennes, 1954), pp. 703-704: "Les notions des corps, de chair, et d'âme, celle-ci conçu comme 'le principle de vie,' c'est tout un."

[83]Robinson, p. 51.

[84]Ibid., pp. 52-53.

[85]Hillman, p. 314.

[86]Robinson, p. 28.

[87]C. Jul. op. imp. I.54.

[88]Frend, Martyrdom and Persecution, p. 348.

[89]Stromata IV.7.43.4; see also II.20.104.

[90]In Ad Uxorem he allows flight in persecution; in De fuga IX.2, he does not: "Infirmos sustineri iubet Paulus, utique enim non fugientes."

[91]Auerbach, Mimesis, p. 69.

[92]De Pallio V.4.55.

[93]Frend, Martyrdom and Persecution, pp. 401-402.

[94]Frend, Ibid., pp. 495-496. We should allow, however, for the paucity of Western sources which may distort Frend's argument here.

[95]Ibid., p. 395.

[96]Homilae in Numeros XXIV.1.

[97]Ibid., X.2; Exhortatio ad Martyrium 36; Contra Celsum III.8.

[98]Contra Celsum IV.17, 18.

[99]Homiliae in Leviticum II.f.

[100]Frend, Martyrdom and Persecution, p. 395.

[101]S. Laeuchli, The Serpent and the Dove (Nashville: Abingdon Press, 1966), p. 110.

[102]Probably between A.D. 325 and 341; C. J. Hefele, History of the Church Councils from the Original Documents, II (Edinburgh: T. & T. Clark, 1876), p. 325.

[103]Laeuchli, pp. 155-156.

[104]Hefele, p. 329.

[105]Laeuchli, p. 198.

[106]Brown, Religion and Society in the Age of St. Augustine (Berkeley: University of California Press, 1972), p. 169.

[107]F. Homes Dudden, The Life and Times of St. Ambrose, II (Oxford: Clarendon Press, 1935), p. 506; Hexaemeron VI.47; Expositio in psalmum CXVIII.10.18; Ep. 72.17.

[108]De Isaac 54.

[109]Dudden, p. 512.

[110]G. B. Ladner has shown that the ascetic teachings of the Cappadocians cannot be easily lumped together: "The Philosophical Anthropology of St. Gregory of Nyssa," Dumbarton Oaks Papers, XII (Cambridge: Harvard University Press, 1958), 61-73.

[111]Ibid., p. 78.

[112]Brown, Religion and Society, p. 201.

[113]P. Courcelle, Recherches sur les Confessions de S. Augustin (Paris: Editions E. de Boccard, 1968), p. 382.

[114]Armstrong, "Neoplatonic Valuations of Nature, Body and Intellect," p. 39.

[115]Noted by Courcelle, Recherches, p. 95; by Dudden, p. 502, and others.

[116]"The unbaptised man is organically united with the devil as his membrum or semen." B. Altaner, Patrology, trans. Hilda Graef (London: Nelson Press, 1958), p. 453.

[117]J. Burnaby, Amor Dei (London: Hodder & Stroughton, 1938), p. 208.

[118]De virginitate II.8; V.23.

[119]Ibid., VII.34.

[120]I have used Peter Brown's dating for De utilitate jejunii, De bono coniungali, and De sancta virginitate; the dating of De continentia is disputed; J. Saint Martin dates it at A.D. 395:396: Introduction to De Continentia, Oeuvres de S. Augustin, 1st Series, vol. III (Paris: Desclée de Brouwer, 1949), p. 17; A.-M. Bonnardière, in "La Date du De Continentia," Revue des Etudes Augustiniennes 1 (1959), places it in A.D. 414-416, contemporaneous with the Pelagian controversy, while D. O'B. Faul, "The Date of the De Continentia of St. Augustine," Studia Patristica 6 (1962): 374, dates it c. A.D. 426. I agree with the Bonnadière dating because of the internal evidence she cites.

[121]De cont. i.1.

[122]Ibid., i.2: "Multa enim corporis ore non dicimus, et corde clamamus."

[123]De cont. vii.17.

[124]Ibid., vii.18.

[125]Ibid., viii.19.

[126]Ibid., iv.10.

[127]De cont. ix.22.

[128]Ibid., x.24; viii.20.

[129]"Corpus quippe ab animi est quidem natura diversum." A more accurate and less misleading translation should read: "of a different nature than the soul."

[130]De cont. xii.26.

[131]Ibid., xiii.28.

[132]De cont. ix.23.

[133]De util. jejun. i.

[134]Ibid., iv.

[135]The fact that this transformation of physical energy to psychical energy is not only possible, but is a verified method of attaining spiritual surcharge, is testified to by numerous writings from the Epic of Gilgamesh to Aldous Huxley's Heaven and Hell. Aldous Huxley, Heaven and Hell (New York: Harper & Row, 1963).

[136] De util. jejun. v.

[137] Ibid., iii.

[138] Ibid., iv.

[139] Ibid., iii.

[140] Ibid., ii.

[141] Ibid., v.

[142] Ibid.

[143] Burnaby, p. 115.

[144] Bourke, pp. 111-112.

[145] Ibid., p. 237.

[146] Burnaby, p. 27.

[147] De cont. viii.19.

[148] John J. Hugo, St. Augustine on Nature, Sex, and Marriage (Chicago: Scepter Press, 1969), p. 31, points out an aspect we must not ignore: this emphasis on procreation as the greatest good of marriage also directly counters Manichaeism.

[149] De bon. con. iii.3.

[150] See Canon 33 of the Synod of Elvira, using this same rationale, had directed a proscription of sexuality for married clergy: "Bishops, presbyters, deacons, and all other clerics having a position in the ministry are ordered to abstain completely from their wives and not to have children." Samuel Laeuchli, Power and Sexuality (Philadelphia: Temple University Press, 1972), p. 130; cf. p. 94.

[151] De bon. con. i.

[152] Ibid., iii.3.

[153] Conf. VI.15.

[154] De bon. con. viii.8.

[155] Ibid., xxiii.28.

[156] De scta. virg. xlvi: "singulis singula."

[157] De bon. con. xxiii.29.

[158] Ibid.

[159] De scta. virg. li.52.

[160]Ibid., xliv.45: ". . . timenti se anteferre non audeat."

[161]Shumacher, p. 130.

[162]G. I. Bonner, "Libido and Concupiscentia in St. Augustine," Studia Patristica, VI (Berlin: Akademie-Verlag, 1962), 303-314.

[163]Ibid., p. 305.

[164]Ibid., p. 308.

[165]In Ps. CXVIII.20; De nupt. et concup. ii.30.52.

[166]Bonner, p. 308.

[167]In Ps. CII.6.

[168]Bonner, p. 310.

[169]Eugene Portalié, A Guide to the Thought of St. Augustine, trans. Bastian (London: Burns & Oates, 1960), p. 208.

[170]Nigel Abercrombie, The Origins of Jansenism (Oxford: Clarendon Press, 1936), p. 18; "The most compromising text, in this connection, is one in which he says that all evil concupiscence may be called fornication, because the soul therein neglects the higher law which governs it, and is corrupted by a base pleasure in its lower nature, as a harlot is corrupted by financial gain (De serm. Dom. I.36). But devotional metaphor is not metaphysical or theological fact."

[171]G. B. Ladner, The Idea of Reform (Cambridge: Harvard University Press, 1959), p. 177.

[172]O'Connell, Early Theory, p. 180.

[173]Bonner, pp. 312-313.

[174]Ibid., p. 313.

[175]F.-J. Thonnard, "La notion de concupiscence chez S. Augustin," Recherches Augustiniennes 3 (1965): 65.

[176]Ibid., p. 64.

[177]O'Connell, Early Theory, p. 190.

[178]Ibid., p. 173; see also Enn. I.8.

[179]O'Connell, Early Theory, p. 173.

[180]In De musica, "il voit un commencement de transformation eschatologique du corps dans l'accroissement de santé et d'harmonie qui se réalise des cette vie lorsque la charité grandit et que diminue la concupiscence." R. Holte, Beatitude et Sagesse: St. Augustin et le problème de la fin de l'Homme dans la

Philosophie Ancienne (Paris: Etudes Augustiniennes, 1962), p. 270; see also De mus. VI.5.13; De vera relig. XLIV.82.

[181]"Ce n'est que l'année suivant, en 394 que, en intensifiant son étude de saint Paul, Augustin découvrit que la lutte entre la chair et l'esprit durent jusqu'à la fin de la vie terrestre." Ibid., p. 271.

[182]A. Sage, "Le Péché Originel dans la Pensée de saint Augustin de 412 à 430," Revue des Etudes Augustiniennes 15 (1969): 91.

[183]Ibid., p. 92; cf. De civ. Dei XIV.3.

[184]Sage, p. 92.

[185]Schumacher, p. 120.

[186]Serm. CXXVIII.9; Serm. CLI.2.

[187]Brown, Augustine of Hippo, p. 391: Both Julian and Augustine "treated their views on sexuality as secondary"; see also C. Jul. op. imp. VI.1.

[188]Norman P. Williams, The Ideas of the Fall and of Original Sin (London: Longmans, Green, 1927), p. 223.

[189]Julian himself understood this to be the position from which Augustine spoke on original sin: C. Jul. op. imp. III.137, 138.

[190]Brown, Augustine of Hippo, p. 354.

[191]E.g., C. Jul. I.4.11; VII.35.

[192]Among the methods used by Augustine and Alypius to secure the suppression of the Italian supporters of Pelagius, Brown lists bribery (C. Jul. op. imp. I.42), denial of free discussion, and exile of bishops (C. Jul. op. imp. I.9); Augustine of Hippo, p. 383.

[193]Brown, Augustine of Hippo, p. 385.

[194]Laeuchli, Power and Sexuality, p. 90.

[195]Ibid., p. 93.

[196]Even in marriage, as Canon 33 of the Synod of Elvira shows.

[197]Laeuchli, Power and Sexuality, p. 95.

[198]De Exhortatione Castitatis vii.

[199]Brown, "Society and the Supernatural."

[200]F. Van der Meer, Augustine the Bishop, trans. Brian Battershaw and G. R. Lamb (London: Sheed & Ward, 1961), pp. 199-234.

[201]Brown, Augustine of Hippo, pp. 384-385; see also C. Jul. VII.31.

[202]Brown, Augustine of Hippo, p. 385; see also C. Jul. V.1.2; VI.20.64; C. Jul. op. imp. II.51.

[203]C. Jul. III.21.42.

[204]Brown, Augustine of Hippo, p. 387.

[205]C. Jul. op. imp. II.1; trans. Brown, Augustine of Hippo, p. 384.

[206]Bonner, "Libido and Concupiscentia," p. 313.

[207]De nupt. et concup. I.1.1.

[208]Cf. Ep. CXXXIV; De civ. Dei XIV.16.21.

[209]De civ. Dei XIV.23.

[210]Brown, Augustine of Hippo, p. 390.

[211]De civ. Dei XIV.16.

[212]"Both generation and birth might have taken place in Paradise sine pudenda libidine . . . si nemo peccasset." C. Jul. op. imp. II.42.

[213]C. Jul. III.7.15.

[214]C. Jul. III.9.18.

[215]Cf. De civ. Dei XIII.14.

[216]Williams, p. 148.

[217]Ibid., p. 461.

[218]C. Jul. op. imp. I.22, 25; De civ. Dei XXII.22.

[219]Williams, p. 357.

[220]C. Jul. IV.7: "Tam magnum est enim malum ejus, ut eo non uti, quam bene uti sit melius."

[221]C. Jul. V.16.62.

[222]C. Jul. V.19.60.

[223]Ibid., III.21.42.

[224]Armstrong, "Neoplatonic Valuations," p. 39.

CHAPTER IV

NOTES

[1]Cochrane, p. 437.

[2]Ibid.

[3]Clark, "Plotinus' Theory of Sensation," p. 357.

[4]Cochrane, p. 437.

[5]H. A. Wolfson, The Philosophy of the Church Fathers (Cambridge: Harvard University Press, 1970), p. 373.

[6]Metaphysics XII.10.1075b.

[7]Wolfson, p. 373; cf. Metaphysics VII.6.1045a.7-8.

[8]De Anima II.1.412a.16-21.

[9]Ibid., I.3.407b.18-21.

[10]Wolfson, p. 380.

[11]Ibid., p. 384.

[12]Long, p. 154.

[13]SVF ii.310; see also Long, p. 154.

[14]Long suggests ingeniously that "following the criterion of existence as 'capable of acting or of being acted upon' . . . body must be analyzable into active and passive components. For it could not simultaneously as a whole both act upon itself and be acted upon by itself" (p. 154). But if there is a true 'mixture' or 'confusion' of elements, one can't see how the purely conceptual analysis of these components would actually render a subject and an object of action.

[15]Spanneut, p. 396.

[16]It is curious to notice the way in which a monistic metaphysical system such as Stoicism compensates with a strong experiential dualism, while a philosophy like Neoplatonism with a marked systematic dualism can acknowledge, perhaps more readily, the final unity.

[17]Pétrement, p. 197.

[18]Puech, p. 265.

[19]Ibid., p. 298.

[20]Brown, Augustine of Hippo, p. 56.

[21]Pétrement, p. 280.

[22]Thomas Whittaker, The Neoplatonists (Hildesheim: George Olms Verlagsbuchhandlung, 1961, 1961), p. 88.

[23]Wallis, p. 73.

[24]Ibid., p. 74; see also Enn. III.6.1-5; I.1; IV.4.18-29.

[25]Wallis, p. 75.

[26]Ibid., p. 29; see also De Anima I.1.403a-b.

[27]Rich, p. 623.

[28]See Rich's discussion, pp. 623ff.

[29]Enn. VI.4.15.

[30]Rich, p. 623.

[31]Ibid.

[32]Ibid., pp. 626-627; see also Enn. IV.3.22.

[33]Rich, p. 629; Enn. III.6.

[34]Enn. I.1.2: "Substantial being is unmixed"; Ἢ τὸ ὀυσιῶ εδ ἄμικτον.

[35]Plotinus also made a curious attempt to isolate and describe a connecting link from the physical side (see discussion of πνεῦμα in Chapter II), which may have been influenced by Galen's discussion of the nerves and the brain (see Rich, pp. 623-633).

[36]Stromata III.7.59.3.

[37]Aloys Grillmeier, Christ in Christian Tradition, trans. J. S. Bowden, 2nd ed. (New York: Sheed & Ward, 1964), I, 138.

[38]De carne Christi 9.

[39]Ibid., 10.

[40]Adversus Praxean 27.

[41]Apologeticum 21.

[42]Adversus Marcionem II.27.

[43]Wolfson demonstrates that Tertullian used the term 'mixture' in its Stoic sense of 'composition' of imperceptible parts; p. 389.

[44]The idea of spirituality of the soul was not totally dominant until a late date; even in the fifth century, not a few ecclesiastical writers taught the materiality of the soul (Fortin, p. 9). The notion of the spirituality of the soul was above all, for the Christians of the first centuries, "une doctrine païenne" (ibid., p. 12).

[45]Contra Celsum III.41;

[46]Wolfson, p. 395.

[47]Ibid., p. 396.

[48]Spanneut, p. 428.

[49]Grillmeier, p. 144, see n. 142.

[50]Dialektos 136.16ff.

[51]Tarsicius J. Van Bavel, Recherches sur la Christologie de Saint Augustin (Fribourg: Editions Universitaires, 1954), p. 1.

[52]Grillmeier, p. 414, cautions against use of the designations 'Alexandrian' and 'Antiochean' in christological controversy before their classical development between A.D. 429 and 451. What we are treating here in the pre-Augustinian fathers, and in Augustine himself, should rather be designated as λόγος-σάρξ and λόγος-ἄνθρωπος, which does not entirely coincide with the usual distinction between 'Alexandrine' and 'Antiochene.' The discussion was over whether Christ was comprised of the Logos 'bonded' to human flesh, or whether a human soul, mind, and will existed in Christ together with λόγος and σάρξ.

[53]Van Bavel describes the two tendencies of christology in the fourth and fifth centuries and their logical results: "Si l'on se base sur la dualité des natures, la nature humaine jouira d'une accentuation qu'elle ne saurait trouvait dans l'autre manière de voir. Elle y paraîtra plus indépendante, disons, plus réaliste. Si l'on met l'accent sur l'unité du Christ l'attention se portera de préférence sur la divinité du Verbe-Incarné. La nature humaine paraîtra comme dominée et pénétrée de l'action et les propriétés divines." Van Bavel, p. 3.

[54]Cochrane, p. 234.

[55]Grillmeier, p. 154.

[56]Ibid., p. 315.

[57]Ibid., p. 368.

[58]Oratio 29.19 (Grillmeier trans., p. 370); see also Gregory of Nyssa, Contra Eunomium V.

[59]Grillmeier, p. 343.

[60]De Isaac 54.

[61]De Incarnationis dominicae sacramento V.56.

[62]De Sacramentis V.16; also V.17: "Remember what I said: 'Christ took on flesh,' not 'as flesh' but that true flesh of yours; Christ truly took on flesh."

[63]Dudden, p. 506.

[64]Enarrationes in Psalmus 61.5; Grillmeier, p. 405.

[65]Grillmeier, p. 405.

[66]Dudden, p. 596.

[67]Grillmeier, p. 400; see Hilary, Tractatus in Psalmus 54.

[68]Grillmeier, p. 401; Jerome, Epistula 120.9.

[69]O'Connell, Early Theory, chap. 10, pp. 258-278.

[70]Van Bavel, p. 168.

[71]But Marrou cautions against imputing too hastily to the Augustine of the Cassiciacum dialogues ignorance of specifically Christian doctrines; he reminds us to consider both the apologetic nature of the dialogues and the effect he wished to attain, which too insistent an emphasis on Christian doctrine would have endangered. It is significant that Alypius did not wish the name of Christ brought into the dialogues; it was primarily to demonstrate the intellectual validity of the Christian faith to friends as well as to a larger circle that Augustine wrote the dialogues. S. Augustin et la fin de la culture antique, p. 244.

[72]De Gen. con. Man. II.24.37.

[73]Conf. VII.19.25.

[74]Augustine transposed "le Logos de Plotin dans les termes du Logos chrêtien précisement parce qu'il ne comprehend pas clairement la doctrine chrêtienne de l'incarnation." M. F. Sciacca, S. Augustin et le Néoplatonisme (Louvain: Publications Universitaires de Louvain, 1956), p. 8.

[75]Conf. VII.19.25.

[76]Van Bavel, p. 11; De ord. II.5.16; De mus. VI.4.7.

[77]"propria sunt mutabilitis animae et mentis."

[78]Conf. VII.19.25.

[79]"profecta Deus," De beata vita xxxiv.

[80]Contra acad. III.43; De ord. II.16; II.25.

[81]De Gen. con. Man. II.56.

[82]Ibid., II.24.37; De vera relig. XVI.31.

[83]"Au temps de jeune Augustin, le mot _persona_ était encore loin d'avoir atteint la signification fixe d'individu rationnel subsistant. . . . A cette époque . . . la signification qui s'impose ici est apparentée à l'usage classique de _persona_ dans le sens de masque de théâtre: tenir la place de quelqu'un, être penétré de celui-ci, en être comme le reflet, la manifestation extérieure, le vêtement, l'aspect, l'apparence." Van Bavel, p. 7.

[84]O'Connell, _Early Theory_, p. 265.

[85]_Retract_. I.18.11.

[86]_De Gen. Con. Man_. II.24.37; _De ag. chr_. 20.22.

[87]See also _Ep_. XIV.3.

[88]_Serm_. CCXIV.6; cf. Grillmeyer, p. 407.

[89]O'Connell, _Early Theory_, p. 267.

[90]Ibid., p. 260.

[91]Ibid., pp. 269-272.

[92]Ibid., p. 268.

[93]He does, however, render understandable Augustine's sometimes strange treatment of the Incarnation in _De vera religione_ by showing its appropriateness in the context of a polemic addressed to the Manichaens (p. 271).

[94]Van Bavel, pp. 1-20.

[95]O'Connell, _Early Theory_, p. 262.

[96]_Conf_. VII.24.

[97]Since Augustine's Incarnational theology is not an overlooked topic, I will not attempt to duplicate or even adumbrate the excellent detailed studies already available.

[98]As John T. Newton, Jr. has suggested, this formula seems to be a direct precursor of the Chalcedon formula; "The Importance of Augustine's Use of the Neoplatonic Doctrine of Hypostatis Union for the Development of Christology," _Augustinian Studies 3_ (1971): 1-16.

[99]With the possible exception of Plotinus.

[100]As Thomas Traherne remarked, centuries later, in _Centuries of Meditation_.

[101]_Ep_. CXXXVII.3.11, dated A.D. 412.

[102]Newton, p. 1.

[103]See above, p. 149; see also Wolfson, pp. 428ff.

[104]Wolfson, p. 399.

[105]Newton, pp. 3,4: The "major Christological texts of Hilary, Ambrose, and Victorinus reveal no use by them of the hypostatic union theory."

[106]In which "nous avons la preuve évidente que saint Augustin garde difficulté à définir le terme persona. . . . Nous sommes ici plus près de la signification 'être la forme révélatrice d'une chose' que du concept moderne de la personne." Van Bavel, pp. 17, 18.

[107]After 411, "on la recontre sous les termes techniquement parfaits de una persona ou in unitate personae au moins soixante-dix fois." Ibid., p. 20.

[108]Ibid., p. 24.

[109]Grillmeier, p. 408.

[110]Fortin, p. 121.

[111]"les deux idées se prêtent un appui mutuel." Ibid., p. 122.

[112]Newton, p. 3; Ep. CXXVIII.1.

[113]"Même si saint Augustin conçoit le composé humaine de la même manière que Plotin, sa pensée n'entraîne pas nécessairement des répercussions néfastes dans le domaine christologique." Van Bavel, p. 22.

[114]"Il ne semble pas . . . qu'Augustin ait modifié essentiellement la doctrine qu'il empruntait aux ennemis du christianisme et dont il se servait pour les confondre. Certes, l'expression, una persona, déjà employée par Tertullian et qu'il retrouve après deux siècles, est bien latine, mais elle ne fait que dire en termes plus précis ce que le grec affirmait déjà à sa façon." Fortin, p. 122. Cf. Tertullian, Adversus Praxean 27.

[115]Cf. Ep. CLXIX.8; Serm. CCXLII; In Joan. Evang. LXXVIII.3; De civ. Dei X.29.2, 34ff; In Joan. Evang. XIX.15 and XLVII.12; Serm. CLXXXVII.3; Serm. CLXXXIX.3.

[116]Ep. CXXXVII.2.11.

[117]As in De civ. Dei X.29.34.

[118]Grillmeier has not adequately described the meaning and function of Augustine's "unity of behavior" in Christ; see Grillmeier, pp. 326-327.

[119]Cf. Nemesius: "the union of soul and body as an extension of the universal soul to the extreme limits"; Grillmeier, p. 390.

[120]I cannot resist an analogy, apposite, I think, in terms of the level of energy, profundity and intensity, with Boris

Vysheslawzeff's description of Aristotle's 'golden mean': "His 'golden mean' has often been misunderstood and disparaged as 'mediocrity.' But Aristotle's 'middle' is a center, a target . . . difficult to hit. . . . Aristotle himself states that this mean does not signify mediocrity, but a summit, an extreme . . . his mean becomes sound and useful only when it dominates and combines two opposing forces or impulses." "Two Ways of Redemption," in The Mystic Vision, ed. J. Campbell (New York: Pantheon Books, 1966), p. 27. Here a basic conflict between distinction and separation comes to light; the uneasiness with 'mixture' of the philosophers led to conceptual separation of elements which must rather be distinguished in order to be 'held together'; Augustine has found a formula which permits distinction of natures and unity of person. With this understanding, mixture is no longer seen as inevitable dilution; from Ep. CXXXVII on, Augustine freely uses the term 'mixture' without pejorative connotations. See Ep. CXXXVII.2, quoted above, p. 157.

[121]". . . jusqu'ici cette grâce a toujours été présentée comme l'état où se trouve le Christ après l'union; tandis que maintenant pour la première fois, c'est l'union elle-même qui est décrite comme une grâce." Van Bavel, pp. 37-38. See also Ep. CLXXVII. 16; In Joan. Evang. CXI.5.

[122]See also Serm. CLXXXIX.3.

[123]I disagree with Grillmeier's judgment that the human soul of Christ becomes not only a 'connecting link' but "it almost becomes a protective screen between the Godhead and the body" (p. 412). The "elevated idea of the spirituality of God" which Augustine has from Neoplatonism implies, as discussed in Chapter II, p. 27, that Augustine will be looking for links between God and man in Christ, not seeking to hold them apart as a materialist would need to do. Grillmeier's evaluation of Augustine's christology seems contradictory; on p. 413 he states: "Latin christology gained much from Augustine. But he could not provide what was needed to bring the crisis which had broken out in the East at the end of his life to a successful outcome"; while on p. 465, in discussing Augustine's instruction to Leporius on the unity and duality of Christ, he writes, "Even Chalcedon at a later date will not have a great deal more to offer."

[124]De fide et symb. IV.10; trans. Grillmeier, p. 412.

[125]"Plus que n'importe quel Père avant lui, saint Augustin insiste sur ce point." Van Bavel, p. 53.

[126]Ep. CXXXVII.3.10.

[127]Markus, Saeculum, pp. 119-120. Interesting and pertinent here is Saul Bellow's statement in Herzog: "Neuroses might be graded by the inability to tolerate ambiguous situations." Saul Bellow, Herzog (New York: Avon Books, 1961), p. 370. See In Ps. CVI: "How many that are not ours as yet, are, as it were, within; and how many that are ours are still, as it were, without. . . . And they that are not ours, who are within, when they find

CHAPTER V

NOTES

[1]*In Ps.* CXXXIV.18.31.

[2]Cf. Portalié, p. 105; Gilson agrees that Augustine's early works "presuppose the doctrine of the immortality of the soul," and adds that "he was never definitely to deny it." *Christian Philosophy of St. Augustine*, pp. 50-51.

[3]P. Brown, *Augustine of Hippo*, p. 366.

[4]The meaning of this struggle is described by C. G. Jung in his autobiography, *Memories, Dreams, and Reflections* (New York: Random House, 1965), p. 302: "A man should be able to say he has done his best to form a conception of life after death, or to create some image of it--even if he must confess his failure. Not to have done so is a vital loss. For the question that is posed to him is the age-old heritage of humanity: an archetype, rich in secret life, which seeks to add itself to our own individual life in order to make it whole."

[5]Chr. Larcher, O.P., "La Doctrine de la Résurrection dans l'ancien test," *Lumière et Vie* 3 (April, 1952): 11.

[6]Ibid., p. 14.

[7]Ibid., p. 34.

[8]J. Schmitt, "La Résurrection de Jésus dans la predication apostolique et la tradition evangélique," *Lumière et Vie* 3 (April 1952): 37; but cf. Matt. 25 for a strong inference in Jesus' teaching of a general resurrection.

[9]L. Cerfaux, "La Résurrection des morts dans la vie et la pensée de s. Paul," *Lumière et Vie* 3 (April, 1952): 74.

[10]H.-I. Marrou, "Le dogme de la résurrection des corps et la théolgie des valeurs humaines selon l'enseignement de saint Augustin," *Revue des Etudes Augustiniennes* 12(1) (1966): 123; hereafter referred to as "Dogme de la résurrection."

[11]A. Nygren, in *Eros and Agape*, claims that Paul was far more important for Augustine than for anyone else in the Early Church. (Philadelphia: Westminster Press, 1953), p. 560.

[12]H.-I. Marrou, "La résurrection des morts et les apologistes des premiers siècles," *Lumière et Vie* 3 (April 1952): 86.

[13]Nygren, p. 287.

[14]Spanneut, p. 95.

their opportunities, go out, and they that are ours, who are without, when they find opportunity, return." Przywara trans., p. 276. Augustine has apparently, in becoming comfortable with 'mixture,' made a decisive step in the direction of psychological vitality, away from dependence on black-and-white evaluations.

[128] In Joan. evang. LXXX.3.

[129] De gen. ad litt. XII.68.

[130] De civ. Dei XIII.6.

[131] c. A.D. 420.

[132] De civ. Dei XV.7.2.

[133] Solil. I.14.24.

[15]Long, Hellenistic Philosophy, p. 213, n. 2.

[16]Tertullian, Adversus Marcionem, V.19; Spanneut, p. 97; see the research of J. M. C. Toynbee on burial practices and tomb ornamentation and inscription which reinforces this point: "there is no hint of any dogma of bodily resurrection for mankind as a whole . . . " Death and Burial in the Roman World (London: Thames & Hudson, 1971), p. 40.

[17]Toynbee, p. 38.

[18]As suggested by Gabriel Marcel: ". . . the problem of death becomes clearer. Is it absolute distraction or does some mode of paying attention to the real still remain possible after the destruction of what I call my body? Yet does not this attention in question imply a center--a point of application--in a word, a body?" Metaphysical Journal (Chicago: Henry Regnery Co., 1952), p. 243. As William J. Wainwright has written: "Being embodied . . . involved apprehending things from a special point of view and occupying a position from which the effects of one's activity radiate outwards in space. It is not clear that these things are imperfections." "God's Body," Journal of the American Academy of Religion 62 (September 1974): 475.

[19]Toynbee, p. 40.

[20]P. Merlan, in CHLGEMP, p. 28.

[21]Phaedo 78C.

[22]Rich, p. 634.

[23]Marrou, "Dogme de la résurrection," p. 117.

[24]"ἡ δ᾽ἀληθινὴ ἐγρήγορσις ἀληθινὴ ἀπὸ σώματος, οὐ μετὰ σώματος, ἀνάστασις."

[25]Armstrong, in CHLGEMP, p. 230.

[26]De civ. Dei XII.16-23; A. H. Armstrong, "St. Augustine and Christian Platonism," Augustine: A Collection of Critical Essays, ed. R. A. Markus (New York: Doubleday Anchor, 1972), p. 13.

[27]One wonders, after reading James Hillman's excellent article, "The Dream and the Underworld" (Eranos Jahrbuch, 1973), how much the teetering superstructure of Plotinus with its spatial imagery of 'up,' balanced--or was a reaction to--the Underworld imagery of classical literature and popular thought. Plotinus seems to have been aware (following Heraclitus, Frag. 62, 88), of the essential identity of "ὁδός τε κατω καὶ ἄνω," the downward and upward way. The body plays no part in either way of imaging death: "Even as late as Ovid, the dead are shades who wander bodiless, bloodless and boneless . . . nature, body, and matter fall away on entering the underworld." Hillman, pp. 259, 272; Metamorphoses IV.5.443.

[28]J. O'Meara, Porphyry's Philosophy from Oracles in Augustine, p. 25.

[29] Ibid., p. 77.

[30] De civ. Dei X.25, 29; XII.26.

[31] Puech, p. 311.

[32] Courcelle, "Propos Antichrétien," p. 163; see also In Ps. LXXXVIII.2.5.

[33] Nygren, p. 283.

[34] C. Journet, "Saint Augustin et l'exégèse traditionelle du 'corpus spirituale,'" Augustinus Magister 2 (1954): 881; cf. Maurice Pontet, L'exégèse de saint Augustin predicateur (Paris: Aubier, 1946), pp. 413-415.

[35] Clement, XXVI.3; Ignatius, Epistula ad Trallianos LX.2; Martyrium Polycarpi XIV.2.

[36] Oratio adversus Graecos 25.

[37] Athenagoras, De resurrectione mortis 15.

[38] This question was dealt with also in rabbinic sources (BT Sanhedrin 91a), as well as in the writings of Zoroaster (Zatspram 34.1.7; David Winston, "The Iranian Component in the Bible," History of Religions 5 (1966): 211.

[39] Pontet, pp. 413-415.

[40] Cf. H. Chadwick, "Origen, Celsus, and the Resurrection of the Body," Harvard Theological Review 41 (1948): 84-102; Wilfred Knox, "Origen's Conception of the Resurrection Body," Journal of Theological Studies 39 (1938): 247-248; Journet, pp. 883-884.

[41] Journet, p. 883.

[42] Chadwick, p. 84. This rationale was used by Clement of Rome (27.2), Justin Martyr (Apologia I.19), Athenagoras (De resurrectione mortis 9), Irenaeus (Adversus Haereses 5.3.2-3), and Tertullian (De carnis resurrectione 57).

[43] He apparently argued that Jesus' body was sui generis as is evident from the virgin birth; Jerome attributes this argument to him (Contra Joannem Hierosolymitanum 26), as does Methodius (Aglaphon, or Discourse on the Resurrection I.26; III.11).

[44] Chadwick, p. 89.

[45] W. Knox, pp. 247-248, has interpreted the passage in De oratione 31.3, in which Origen discusses ἐπουρανίων τα σῶματα as implying that "only the divine element in man survives." He finds this doctrine derived from Timaeus 33b where "the spherical shape of the human head aptly represents the fact that it is the most divine element in us that controls the whole," and logically implies "that the resurrection body, being spherical, would be merely a permanent survival of the spherical element . . . the ἡγεμονικόν in the soul of man." But Chadwick argues that a

superficial reading of this passage has led to that interpretation; he disputes that this was Origen's view since neither Methodius nor Jerome accuses him of it and it appears only in Origen's sixth-century followers who were anathematized at the Council of Constantinople in A.D. 543. See Chadwick, pp. 101-102.

[46]Concentrated in De principiis II.10; III.4; Contra Celsum II.77; V.18, 22, and 23.

[47]See also A. Chollet, "Corps Glorieux," Dictionnaire de Théologie Catholique, III, c. 1895; Journet, p. 883; Chadwick, pp. 98-99; Knox, pp. 247-248.

[48]Journet, p. 883.

[49]Methodius' On the Resurrection is a polemic against Origen's views of the resurrection. See esp. I.13; II.13: "There is no resurrection of the form without the flesh." Hilary, Tractatus super Psalmos II.41; LV.12; XLV.12; Epiphanius, Ancoratus LXXXVII and XC; Expositio fidei XVII, XVIII.

[50]Journet, p. 886; Gregory of Nyssa, De anima et resurrectione; In Christi resurrectionem, Oratio III.

[51]Journet, p. 887.

[52]John Chrysostom, Epistula ad I Corinthianum 41.3.

[53]In addition, it may be an unwarranted oversimplification to schematize views on the resurrection body as 'spiritualizing' and 'concretizing' orientations. In fathers like Gregory of Nyssa and Hilary, for example, where we find the 'spiritual' view maximized, we also find a corresponding, sometimes exaggerated insistence on the concreteness and identity of the resurrection body, so that there is an intensification of both rather than an emphasis on one to the detriment of the other. Cf. G. B. Ladner's article, "The Philosophical Anthropology of Gregory of Nyssa," p. 62, as teaching the "excellence and dignity" of both the human mind and body, the result of a "twofold spiritual inheritance," the Pauline idea of the body as the temple of God, and the Greek effort to attain καλοκάγαθία, a balance of physical and moral perfection.

[54]DTC XIII.2, col. 2539.

[55]In Epistula ad Eph. V.29; Adversus Jovinianum I.36.

[56]Contra Joannem Hierosolymitanum II.33.xxiii.

[57]In Psalmus I.51; cf. In Lucam X.168, 170.

[58]O'Connell, Early Theory, p. 204.

[59]". . . the well-known argument drawn from the subsistence of truth. Truth is naturally indestructible; therefore the soul, which is the subject of truth, must be indestructible as well." Gilson, The Christian Philosophy of St. Augustine, p. 51; Solil. II.19.33; Ep. III.4; De immort. anim. 1-6.

[60]Brown, *Augustine of Hippo*, pp. 146-147; see also *De serm. Dom. in monte* I.2.9.

[61]See above, p. 102.

[62]O'Connell, *Early Theory*, p. 236.

[63]*De quant. anim*. XXIII.76.

[64]Ibid.

[65]Jung's term for such universal experience is 'archetypal,' in this case, the rising of the sun.

[66]*De quant. anim*. XXIII.76.

[67]Cf. Christine Mohrmann, "Saint Augustin écrivain," *Recherches Augustiniennes* 1 (1958): 52.

[68]*De Gen. ad. litt*. VI.24.

[69]Ibid., trans. Ladner, *Idea*, p. 157.

[70]Ibid., p. 158.

[71]*Contra Faust. Mani*. XIV.2.

[72]*De cons. Evang*. IV.10.20. Trans. Peter Brown, *Augustine of Hippo*, p. 147; see *De civ. Dei* XXII.30.49ff; *De corr. et grat*. xii.33.

[73]See Marrou's discussion of the interweaving of philosophical and biblical usage in "Dogme de résurrection," p. 121.

[74]Concluding that it is Christ "per quem vivendi exemplum nobis daretur, hoc est via certa qua perveniremus ad Deum."

[75]*De fide et symb*. X.24.

[76]Ibid., X.24; cf. *De mus*. VI.4.7. In his notes to *De musica* VI in the *Oeuvres de saint Augustin*, VII, F.-J. Thonnard writes that the resurrection, involving the perfecting of the soul in its union with the body, "c'est un point de la foi catholique que s. Augustin semblait oublier dans le *De musica*" (p. 516).

[77]H.-I.Marrou, "Synesius of Cyrene and Alexandrian Neoplatonism," in *The Conflict between Paganism and Christianity in the Fourth Century*, ed. Arnaldo Momigliano (Oxford: Clarendon, 1963), p. 146; see also Origen, *Contra Celsum* vii.36-38.

[78]c. A.D. 408.

[79]c. A.D. 413.

[80]D: J. Leahy, *St. Augustine on Eternal Life* (New York: Benziger Bros., 1939), p. 100.

[81]Written between A.D. 425 and 427.

[82]We must not forget how pressing this conflict was in North Africa in Augustine's time. W. Frend points out that the African clergy were "continually suspected of Manichaeism," that there is "evidence to suggest that a certain amount of secret Manichaeism persisted within the Catholic Church, and Augustine himself was accused of still being a Manichee on the eve of his ordination in the letter of Megalius to Valerius. Frend, "Manichaeism in the Struggle between Saint Augustine and Petilian of Constantine," _Augustinus Magister_, II, 862-865.

[83]c. A.D. 397-398.

[84]_Contra Faust. Mani_. XI.3.

[85]Ibid.

[86]Marrou, "Dogme de la résurrection," p. 115, n. 20.

[87]See Marrou's lengthy listing of citations of Augustine's recurring statement that "the specific and fundamental belief of Christians, which distinguishes them from pagans and Jews, is faith in the resurrection of Christ." "Dogme de la résurrection," p. 114, n. 16.

[88]_Serm_. XXII.10.10, Przywara trans., _An Augustine Synthesis_, p. 295.

[89]Van Bavel discusses Augustine's treatment of Romans 14: "Il se contente d'une solution théologiquement bien pauvre: le Fils de Dieu est prédestiné à la résurrection, parce que la résurrection est une oeuvre divine." pp. 190-191.

[90]_De fide et symb_. VI. S. D. F. Salmond, trans., _A Select Library of the Nicene and Post-Nicene Fathers_, III, 326.

[91]See Marrou's list of citations on Christ as _exemplum_: "Dogme de la résurrection," p. 114, n. 18.

[92]_Serm_. CCXIII.9.

[93]Armstrong, in Markus, ed., p. 11.

[94]_Ep_. LV.21.

[95]_De Trin_. XI.1.

[96]_Ep_. LV.6.10; 5.8; see _In Ps_. LXXXVIII.38; LXXI.7; X.3.4.

[97]_De civ. Dei_ XIII.24.

[98]_Enarr. in Ps_. CXLV.3.

[99]_Serm_. CCXL.3.

[100]_In Ps_. LXIII.9; _In Ps_. CXXII.12; CXLVI.6; _Serm_. CCLXXVIII. 5.

[101]*De civ. Dei* XXII.21.30.

[102]Thomas E. Clarke, S.J., "St. Augustine and Cosmic Redemption," *Theological Studies* 19(2) (1958): 159. Clarke says that Augustine's terminology in the interpretation of I Corinthians 7:31 is close enough to that of Irenaeus "to suggest a direct borrowing." See also *Adversus haereses* V.36.1.

[103]Clarke, p. 160; see also *De civ. Dei* XX.16; *Ep*. CXLVII. 20.48; and *Ep*. CXLVIII.5.16.

[104]Cf. John H. S. Burleigh, *The City of God: A Study in St. Augustine's Philosophy* (London: Nisbet, 1949), p. 122: "St. Augustine pits the naturalists against the philosophers, the known or alleged facts of observation against the theories of deductive physics."

[105]*De civ. Dei* XXI.7.

[106]Ibid., XXI.10.

[107]Ibid., XXI.8.

[108]Ibid., XXII.8.

[109]As Ladner has shown (*The Idea of Reform*, p. 157), this view is in contrast with that of Origen, "for whom the body of Adam at its first creation was as spiritualized as the bodies of all men will be after their resurrection." See Origen, *De principiis*, *In Leviticum* VI.2.

[110]*De Gen. ad litt*. VI.24.

[111]Schumacher, p. 193.

[112]*Enchir*. XCI.

[113]*Serm*. CCXLII.8.11.

[114]Ibid., CCXLIII.9; *De civ. Dei* XXII.30.1.

[115]*De civ. Dei* XXII.21.

[116]Ibid., XXII.29.4; XXII.21.

[117]We will not treat these objections here; they are dealt with in many places by Augustine; especially see *Serm*. CCXLII. 3.4; *Serm*. CCCLXI and CCLXII.39; *Enchir*. LXXXIV to XCII; *De civ. Dei* XXII.5, 12, 45.

[118]*Serm*. CCXLIII.7.

[119]*Enchir*. XCI.

[120]*Serm*. CCXLIII.9.

[121]*De civ. Dei* XIII.2; *Serm*. CCXLII.2.2.

[122]The discussion, p. 111 above, concerning Augustine's changing view of whether the vision of God will be with the eyes of the body, is also relevant to this point.

[123]*Serm*. CCXLIII.8.

[124]See above, p. 165, n. 43.

[125]*Serm*. CCCLXI.15.15. See also *Sermo Mai* LXXXVII.1-2.

[126]*Serm*. CCXL.2. See also *Serm*. CCXLI.1; *Serm*. CCLXXVII. 8.15; *De civ. Dei* X.29.

[127]Van Bavel, pp. 54-55.

[128]*Ep*. CCV.1.

[129]*In Ps*. CXXV.2, trans. Pryzwara.

[130]See above, p. 110.

[131]*Enchir*. XCI; An almost identical treatment appears in *Ep*. CCV.2.

[132]Hillman, p. 283.

[133]*De civ. Dei*. XIII.3.

[134]*De excessu Sat*. II.39; Dudden, p. 512.

[135]*De civ. Dei* XIII.6.

[136]"asperum sensum et contra naturam."

[137]*De Gen. ad litt*. XII.25.68.

[138]*Serm*. CCXLI.4, 6.

[139]*De civ. Dei* XIII.19. See also *Serm*. CCLXXXI.5; *De civ. Dei* XXII.26.

[140]*De doct. christ*. I.24.24. See also *De civ. Dei* XIII.16; *In Ps*. CXLI.18; *De cura pro mortuis gerenda* VII.9.

[141]"instrumentum fieret, per quod transiretur ad vitam." *De civ. Dei* XIII.5.

[142]"pie fideliterque tolerando . . . non aufert vocabulum poenae." Ibid., XIII.6.

[143]Marcel, p. 41.

[144]Abraham Maslow has characterized these as regressive, or fear-choices, and progressive, or growth-choices. *The Farther Reaches of Human Nature* (New York: Viking Press, 1971), p. 23.

[145]Pétrement, p. 34.

[146]E. Gilson's wonderfully apt phrase with which he characterizes Augustine's entire endeavor. Gilson, Christian Philosophy, p. 227.

[147]Pétrement, p. 342.

[148]Ibid., p. 343.

[149]Gilson, Christian Philosophy, p. 4.

[150]We may recall Pétrement's observation, mentioned above, p. 6, of the 'coincidence' of dualistic tendencies in old age in both Plato and Augustine. Plotinus may also be used as an example here; in youth and maturity his writings are mostly on "the beauty of the intellectual world and ecstasy . . ." (Hadot, p. 91); in old age, he wrote "almost exclusively on moral subjects."

[151]Conf. VII.14, 16; De vera relig. XXII.43.

[152]Marrou, p. 126; see In Ps. CXXVIII.16; De Trin. IV.3.5.

[153]De civ. Dei XIII.10.

[154]Van Bavel, p. 137; see De pecc. mer. et rem. II.31.51 (A.D. 412); C. Jul. op. imp VI.40 (A.D. 429-430).

[155]Van Bavel, p. 136; In Ps. XXXII.2.2.

[156]In Joan. Evang. CXXIII.5; Serm. CCXCIX.8, 9; Serm. CCXVII.2, 3.

[157]Conf. X.7.2: "transibo et istam uim meam qua haereo corpori et vitaliter compagem eius repleo."

[158]Serm. CCCXLIV.4, trans. P. Brown, Augustine of Hippo, p. 40.

[159]Cf. Charles Couturier, S.J., "La structure metaphysique de l'homme d'après saint Augustin," pp. 549-550. But Couturier's claim to see in this a 'dépendance instrumentale' goes too far. See also In Joan. Evang. XIV.1,2.

[160]De civ. Dei XXII.24.1.

[161]Ibid., XXII.24.2.

[162]De civ. Dei XXII.30: "This is the picture suggested to my mind . . . Admoneor etiam . . . "

[163]See also Retract. I.2.4; see Ragnar Holte's discussion of Augustine's development in his conception of the beata vita. Holte, pp. 270-271.

[164]In Joan. Evang. XXIII.6; trans. J. Burnaby, Amor Dei, p. 27.

CHAPTER VI

NOTES

[1]*De civ. Dei* XXII.26; See Tertullian, *De resurrectione carnis* vii.

[2]But cf. *Mysterium Conjunctionis*, pp. 467-468, where Jung says that the dogma of the resurrection of the body "remains at the second anticipatory stage of the *conjunctio*, the union of *unio mentalis* with the body." My use of these concepts of Jungian analysis to illuminate Augustine's work seems to parallel Augustine's use of Neoplatonic insights to illuminate Christian ideas. But in doing history, far more important than any particular framework of ideas, is attention to the statement of Freud which I have kept above my desk during the writing of this dissertation as an invaluable reminder: "I learned to restrain speculative tendencies and to look at the same things again and again until they themselves begin to speak." *History of the Psychoanalytic Movement*, Vol. XIV of *The Complete Psychological Works of Sigmund Freud* (London: Hogarth Press, 1957), p. 22.

[3]"Is not our absorbing love of life really the soul's love for its body, a love which will haunt it until that body is returned to it risen and glorious?" *De Gen. ad litt*. XII.35.68.

[4]*Serm*. XXX.4.6; Przywara trans., p. 424.

[5]*Ep*. CXVIII.3.14.

[6]Freud, *Collected Papers*, ed. J. Riviere and J. Strachey (London: International Psychoanalytical Press, 1924-50), V, 182.

[7]E. R. Dodds, p. 54, n. 2; see the discussion in Chapter III of this dissertation.

[8]*Heraclidis Paradeisos* I.

[9]Armstrong, p. 10.

[10]Brown, *Augustine of Hippo*, p. 393.

[11]*C. Jul*. IV.13.71.

[12]Brown, *Augustine of Hippo*, p. 389.

[13]See *De civ. Dei* XIV.16, cited above, p. 74; also *De nupt. et concup*. I.24.27.

[14]This is the emphasis in Augustine's description of his daily struggle against *concupiscentia* in eating and drinking: *Conf*. X.3.

[15]In Joan. Evang. XXIII.10.

[16]Ep. CXXXVII.2.5.

[17]Conf. VII.17.

[18]Cf. Yoga instruction to withdraw the vital energy slowly from the different parts of the body and to concentrate it in the back of the head. Compare also Enn. V.3.17: "How shall we find the way? What method can we devise? How can one see the inconceivable Beauty which stays within the holy sanctuary and does not come out where the profane can see it? Let him who can follow and come within and leave outside the sight of his eyes and not turn back to the bodily splendors which he saw before. When he sees the beauty of bodies he must not run after them; we must . . . hurry away to that which they image." Armstrong trans. (London: George Allen & Unwin, 1953), p. 136.

[19]Conf. VII.17; IX.10.

[20]Conf. X.6. Cf. De lib. arb. II.20.54; II.16.41-42, 44; De Trin. VII.3.4-5; Ix.6.9-10; Serm. CCXLI.2.2; 3.3.

[21]Serm. CLV.15.

[22]H. C. Puech, "Concept of Redemption of Manichaeism," article cited, has emphasized the psychological-experiential basis of Gnostic theory, p. 249.

BIBLIOGRAPHY

I. Primary Sources

A. Augustine

I have used the following abbreviations in referring to the works of Augustine. Volume numbers of J. P. Migne, *Patrologiae Cursus Completus*, Series Latina (Paris, 1844-1864), are indicated.

		PL
Conf.	*Confessionem Libri* XIII	xxxii
Cont. acad.	*Contra Academicos*	xxxii
Contra duas epist. Pelag.	*Contra duas epistolas Pelagianorum*	xlii
Contra Faust. Mani.	*Contra Faustum Manichaeum*	xlii
C. Jul.	*Contra Julianum haeresis Pelagianae defensorem*	xliv
C. Jul. op. imp.	*Contra Julianum opus imperfectum*	xlv
De ag. chr.	*De agone christiano*	xl
De anim et ejus orig.	*De anima et ejus origine*	xliv
	De beata vita	xxxii
De bon. con.	*De bono conjungali*	xl
De civ. Dei	*De civitate Dei*	xl, xli, xlii, xliv
De cons. Evang.	*De consensu Evangelistarum*	xxxiv
De cont.	*De continentia*	xl
De corr. et grat.	*De correptione et gratia*	xliv
De cura pro mort.	*De cura pro mortius gerenda*	xl
De div. quaest.	*De diversus quaestionibus ad Simplicianum*	xl
De doct. christ.	*De doctrina christiana*	xxxiv
De fide et symb.	*De fide et symbolo*	xl

De Gen. ad litt.	De Genesi ad litteram	xxxiv
De Gen. contra Man.	De Genesi contra Manichaeos	xxxiv
De immort. anim.	De immortalitate animae	xxxii
De lib. arb.	De libero arbitrio	xxxii
De mor. Eccl. cath.	De moribus Ecclesiae catholicae	xxxii
De mor. Eccl. Mani.	De moribus Ecclesiae Manichaeorum	xxxii
De mus.	De musica	xxxii
De nat. et grat.	De natura et gratia	xliv
De nupt. et concup.	De nuptiis et concupiscentia	xliv
De opere mon.	De opere monachorum	xl
De pecc. mer. et rem.	De peccatorum meritis et remissione et de baptismo parulorum	xliv
De quant. anim.	De quantitate animae	xxxii
De scta. virg.	De sancta virginitate	xl
De serm. Dom. in monte	De sermone Domini in monte	xliii
De Trin.	De Trinitate	xlii
De util. cred.	De utilitate credendi	xlii
De util. jejun.	De utilitate jejunii	xl
De vera relig.	De vera religione	xxxiv
Enchir.	Enchiridion ad Laurentium sive de fide, spe et caritate	xl
Ep.	Epistulae	xxxiii
Exp. inch. ad Rom.	Expositio 84 propositionem epistolae ad Romanos	xxxv
In Joan. Evang.	In Joannis Evangelium tractus	xxv
In Ps.	Enarrationes in Psalmos	xxxvi
Retract.	Retractationes	xxxii
Serm.	Sermones	xxxviii, xxxix
Solil.	Soliloquia	xxxii

B. Other

Works of most classical, Patristic, and medieval authors are cited in their full Latin title in footnotes. Translations of Patristic authors are from The Fathers of the Church Series unless otherwise indicated.

Early Stoic quotations are from Stoicorum Veterum Fragmenta, ed. H. Von Arnim (Leipzig, 1903-1924; repr. Stuttgart, 1964). Footnotes cite translations used.

C. Translations

I have used the English translations cited below for specific works of Augustine. For works other than these, I have used The Fathers of the Church (Washington, D.C.: Catholic University of America, 1947-) unless specifically indicated in notes.

Augustine:

The Confessions of St. Augustine. Translated by Rex Warner. New York: New American Library; a Mentor-Omega Book, 1963.

City of God. Translated by Henry Bettenson. New York: Penguin Books, 1972.

The Enchiridion on Faith, Hope and Love. Translated by J. B. Shaw. Chicago: Henry Regnery, 1961.

Of True Religion. Translated by J. H. S. Burleigh. Chicago: Henry Regnery, 1968.

Collections of Selected Passages:

An Augustine Synthesis. Arranged by Erich Przywara. New York: Harper & Row; Harper Torchbooks, 1958.

Plotinus:

Enneads I-III. Translated by A. H. Armstrong. 3 vols. Cambridge: Harvard University Press; Loeb Classical Library, 1966.

Enneads IV-VI. Translated by Stephen MacKenna. New York: Pantheon Books, 1962.

II. Secondary Works

Abercrombie, Nigel. The Origins of Jansenism. Oxford: Clarendon Press, 1936.

Altaner, B. Patrology. Translated by Hilda Graef. London: Nelson Press, 1958.

Armstrong, A. H. "Neoplatonic Valuations of Nature, Body, and Intellect." Augustinian Studies 3 (1972).

________. "St. Augustine and Christian Platonism." In Augustine: A Collection of Critical Essays. Edited by R. A. Markus. New York: Doubleday Anchor Press, 1972.

Auerbach, Eric. Literary Language and Its Public in Late Latin Antiquity and in the Middle Ages. London: Kegan Paul, 1965.

________. Mimesis: The Representation of Reality in Western Literature. Princeton: Princeton University Press, 1953.

Baguette, Charles. "Une periode stoicienne dans l'évolution de la pensée de saint Augustin." Revue des Etudes Augustiniennes 16 (1970).

Beckaert, J. A. "Bases Philosophiques de l'ascèse augustinienne." Augustinus Magister 2 (1954).

Bonnardière, A.-M. "La date du 'De Concupiscentia' de saint Augustin." Revue des Etudes Augustiniennes 1 (1959).

Bonner, G. I. "Libido and Concupiscentia in St. Augustine." Studia Patristica 6 (1962).

Bonsirven, J. L'Evangile de Paul. Aubier: Editions Montaigne, 1948.

Bourke, Vernon J. Augustine's Quest of Wisdom. Milwaukee: Bruce Publishing Co., 1945.

Brown, Peter. Augustine of Hippo. Berkeley: University of California Press, 1967.

________. Religion and Society in the Age of St. Augustine. New York: Harper & Row, 1972.

________. "Society and the Supernatural." Unpublished lectures presented at the University of California, Berkeley, January 1975.

Buckenmeyer, Robert E. "St. Augustine and the Life of Man's Body in the Early Dialogues." Augustinian Studies 3 (1972).

Burnaby, J. Amor Dei. London: Hodder & Stoughton, 1938.

Cambridge History of Later Greek and Early Medieval Philosophy. Edited by A. H. Armstrong. Cambridge: University Press, 1970.

Cerfaux, L. "La Résurrection de Jésus dans la predication apostolique et la tradition evangélique." Lumière et Vie 3 (1952).

Chadwick, H. "Origen, Celsus, and the Resurrection of the Body." Harvard Theological Review 41 (1948).

Chollet, A. "Corps Glorieux." Dictionnaire de Théologie Catholique, vol. 3, c. 1895.

Clark, G. H. "Plotinus' Theory of Sensation." Philosophical Review 51 (1942).

Clarke, Thomas E. "St. Augustine and Cosmic Redemption." Theological Studies 19 (1958).

Cochrane, C. N. Christianity and Classical Culture. New York: Oxford University Press, 1940.

Courcelle, Pierre. "Propos antichrétiens rapportés par saint Augustin." Recherches Augustiniennes 1 (1958).

________. Recherches sur les Confessions de saint Augustin. Paris: Editions E. de Boccard, 1968.

Dodds, E. R. Pagan and Christian in an Age of Anxiety. New York: W. W. Norton, 1965.

Dudden, F. Homes. The Life and Times of St. Ambrose. 2 vols. Oxford: Clarendon Press, 1935.

Evans, Ernest. Tertullian's Treatise on the Incarnation. London: S.P.C.K., 1956.

Fortin, E. L. Christianisme et Culture Philosophique au Cinquième Siècle. Paris: Etudes Augustiniennes, 1959.

Frend, W. H. C. "Gnostic-Manichaean Tradition in Roman North Africa." Journal of Ecclesiastical History 4 (1953).

________. "Manichaeism in the Struggle between St. Augustine and Petilian of Constantine." Augustinus Magister 2 (1954).

________. Martyrdom and Persecution in the Early Church. Oxford: Basil Blackwell, 1965.

Gannon, Sister Mary Ann Ida. "The Active Theory of Sensation in St. Augustine." The New Scholasticism 30 (1956).

Gilson, Etienne. The Christian Philosophy of St. Augustine. New York: Random House, 1960.

________. The Christian Philosophy of St. Thomas Aquinas. Translated by L. K. Shook. New York: Random House, 1956.

Grillmeier, Aloys. Christ in Christian Tradition. 2nd ed. Atlanta: John Knox Press, 1975.

Guitton, Jean. The Modernity of St. Augustine. Baltimore: Helicon Press, 1959.

Hadot, Pierre. Plotin ou la simplicité du regard. Paris: Librairie Plon, 1963.

Hefele, C. J. A History of the Christian Councils from the Original Documents. Edinburgh: T. & T. Clark, 1871-76.

Holman, Sister Mary J. Nature Imagery in the Works of St. Augustine. Dissertation submitted to the Catholic University of America. Washington, D.C.: Catholic University of America, Patristic Series XXXIII, 1931.

Holte, Ragnar. Béatitude et Sagesse: St. Augustin et le problème de la fin de l'homme dans la philosophie ancienne. Paris: Etudes Augustiniennes, 1962.

Hugo, John J. St. Augustine on Nature, Sex, and Marriage. Chicago: Scepter Press, 1969.

Jones, A. H. M. The Later Roman Empire II. Oxford: Blackwell, 1964.

Journet, Charles. "Saint Augustin et l'exégèse traditionelle du 'corpus spirituale,'" Augustinus Magister 2 (1954).

Jungmann, J. A. The Early Liturgy. Notre Dame: University of Notre Dame Press, 1959.

Knox, Wilfred. "Origen's Conception of the Resurrection Body." Journal of Theological Studies 39 (1938).

Ladner, G. B. The Idea of Reform. Cambridge: Harvard University Press, 1959.

________. "The Philosophical Anthropology of St. Gregory of Nyssa." Dumbarton Oaks Papers 12 (1958).

Laeuchli, Samuel. Power and Sexuality: The Emergence of Canon Law at the Synod of Elvira. Philadelphia: Temple University Press, 1972.

________. The Serpent and the Dove. New York: Abingdon Press, 1966.

Larcher, Charles. "La doctrine de la résurrection dans l'ancien testament." Lumière et Vie 3 (1952).

Leahy, D. J. St. Augustine on Eternal Life. New York: Benziger Bros., 1939.

Long, A. A. Hellenistic Philosophy. New York: Charles Scribner's Sons, 1974.

Markus, R. A. "Alienatio: Philosophy and Eschatology in the Development of an Augustinian Idea." Studia Patristica 9 (1966).

________. "The Inner Man." Augustine: A Collection of Critical Essays. New York: Doubleday, 1972.

________. "Marius Victorinus and Augustine." In Cambridge History of Later Greek and Early Medieval Philosophy. Edited by A. H. Armstrong. Cambridge: University Press, 1970.

________. "Saeculum: History and Society in the Theology of St. Augustine. Cambridge: University Press, 1970.

Marrou, H.-I. "Le dogme de la résurrection des corps et la théologie des valeurs humaines selon l'enseignement de saint Augustin." Revue des Etudes Augustiniennes 12 (1966).

________. "La résurrection des morts et les apologistes des premiers siècles." Lumière et Vie 3 (1952).

________. St. Augustin et la fin de la culture antique. Paris: Etudes Augustiniennes, 1959.

Martindale, C. C. "A Sketch of the Life and Character of St. Augustine." St. Augustine: His Life and Thought. New York: World Publishing Co., 1957.

Mohrmann, C. "Saint Augustin écrivain." Recherches Augustiniennes 1 (1958).

Momigliano, Arnaldo. The Conflict Between Paganism and Christianity in the Fourth Century. Oxford: Clarendon Press, 1963.

Nash, Ronald H. The Light of the Mind: St. Augustine's Theory of Knowledge. Lexington: University of Kentucky Press, 1969.

Newton, John T. "The Importance of Augustine's Use of the Neoplatonic Doctrine of Hypostatic Union for the Development of Christology." Augustinian Studies 3 (1971).

Nygren, A. Eros and Agape. Philadelphia: Westminster Press, 1953.

O'Connell, Robert J. "De libero arbitrio: Stoicism Revisited." Augustinian Studies 1 (1970).

________. St. Augustine's Early Theory of Man. Cambridge: Harvard University Press, 1968.

O'Meara, John J. Porphyry's Philosophy from Oracles in Augustine. Paris: Etudes Augustiniennes, 1959.

Pétrement, Simone. Le Dualisme chez Platon, les Gnostiques et les Manichéens. Paris: Presses Universitaires de France, 1947.

Pontet, M. L'éxègese de S. Augustin, prédicateur. Paris: Aubier, 1946.

Portalié, Euguene. A Guide to the Thought of St. Augustine. Translated by R. J. Bastian. London: Burns & Oates, 1960.

Prat, . Théologie de saint Paul. 3rd ed. Paris: Beauchesne, 1913.

Puech, H.-C. "The Concept of Redemption in Manichaeism." In The Mystic Vision. Edited by J. Campbell. New Jersey: Princeton University Press, 1968.

Rich, A. N. M. "Body and Soul in the Philosophy of Plotinus." Journal of the History of Philosophy I (1963).

Rist, J. M. Plotinus: The Road to Reality. Cambridge: University Press, 1967.

Robinson, J. A. T. The Body: A Study in Pauline Theology. London: SCM Press, 1952.

Rohmer, J. "L'intentionalité des sensations chez S. Augustin." Augustinus Magister 1 (1954).

Sage, A. "Le Péché originel dans la pensée de saint Augustin de 412 à 430." Revue des Etudes Augustiniennes 15 (1969).

Schmitt, J. "La résurrection de Jésus dans la prédication apostolique et la tradition evangélique." Lumière et Vie 3 (1952).

Schumacher, Wm. A. Spiritus and Spiritualis: A Study in the Sermons of St. Augustine. Mundelein, Illinois: St. Mary of the Lake Seminary Press, 1957.

Sciacca, M. F. S. Augustin et le Néoplatonisme. Louvain: Publications Universitaires de Louvain, 1956.

Solignac, A. "Notes." Oeuvres de saint Augustin, De Genesi ad litteram VII-XII. Series VII, vol. 49. Paris: Desclée de Brouwer, 1972.

Spanneut, Michel. Le Stoïcisme des Pères de l'Église de Clément de Rome à Clément d'Alexandrie. Paris: Université de Paris, 1957.

Testard, Maurice. S. Augustin et Ciceron. 2 vols. Paris: Etudes Augustiniennes, 1958.

Thonnard, R. P. "Notes." Oeuvres de saint Augustin, De musica. Series I, vol. 7. Paris: Desclée de Brouwer, 1947.

________. "La notion de concupiscence en philosophie augustinienne." Recherches Augustiniennes 3 (1965).

Toynbee, J. M. C. Death and Burial in the Roman World. London: Thames & Hudson, 1971.

Van Bavel, Tarsicius J. Recherches sur la christologie de saint Augustin. Fribourg: Editions Universitaires, 1954.

Verbeke, G. L'évolution de la doctrine du pneuma du Stoïcisme à S. Augustin. Paris: Desclée de Brouwer, 1945.

Wainright, William J. "God's Body." Journal of the American Academy of Religion 42 (1974).

Wallis, R. T. Neoplatonism. New York: Charles Scribner's Sons, 1972.

Williams, N. P. The Ideas of the Fall and of Original Sin. London: Longmans, Green, 1927.

Winston, David. "The Iranian Component in the Bible." History of Religions 5 (1966).

Wolfson, H. A. The Philosophy of the Church Fathers. Cambridge: Harvard University Press, 1970.

III. Additional Secondary Works

Bachelard, Gaston. The Poetics of Space. New York: Orion Press, 1964.

Bellow, Saul. Herzog. New York: Avon Books, 1961.

Campbell, Joseph, ed. The Mystic Vision, Eranos. Princeton: Princeton University Press, 1966.

________. The Mythic Image. Princeton: Princeton University Press, 1974.

Custance, J. Wisdom, Madness, and Folly. New York: Pellegrini & Cudahy, 1952.

Freud, S. Collected Papers. Edited by J. Riviere and J. Strachey. London: International Psychoanalytic Press, 1924-1950.

________. The Complete Psychological Works of Sigmund Freud. Vol. 14: On the History of the Psychoanalytic Movement. London: Hogarth Press, 1957.

Hillman, James. "The Dream and the Underworld." Eranos 42 (1973).

________. "The Language of Psychology and the Speech of the Soul." In The Mystic Vision, Eranos. Edited by J. Campbell. Princeton: Princeton University Press, 1966.

Huxley, Aldous. Heaven and Hell. New York: Harper & Row, 1963.

Jung, C. G. Memories, Dreams and Reflections. New York: Random House, 1965.

________. Mysterium Conjunctionis. New York: Bollingen Series XX, 1963.

________. The Structure and Dynamics of the Psyche. New York: Bollingen Series VIII, 1962.

________. Über psychische Energetik und das Wesen der Traum. Zurich: Rasher, 1948. English translation, Two Essays on Analytical Psychology. New York: Bolingen Series VII, 1953.

Marcel, Gabriel. Metaphysical Journal. Translated by Bernard Wall. Chicago: Henry Regnery, 1952.

Maslow, Abraham. The Farther Reaches of Human Nature. New York: Viking Press, 1971.

O'Kelly, Bernard. The Renaissance Image of Man and the World. Columbus: Ohio State University Press, 1966.

Ornstein, Robert. The Psychology of Consciousness. New York: Penguin Books, 1972.

Piaget, Jean. The Construction of Reality in the Child. New York: Ballantine Books, 1954.

Rilke, Rainer Maria. The Notebooks of Malte Laurids Brigge. Translated by M. D. Herter Norton. New York: W. W. Norton, 1949.

Ward, M., ed. France Pagan? New York: Sheed & Ward, 1949.

I. General Index

II. Index of Augustinian Passages